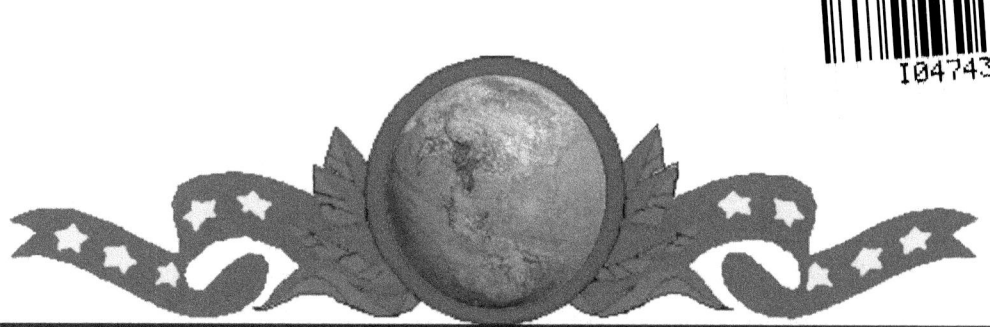

Real World
Colouring Book
For Advanced Users & Adults

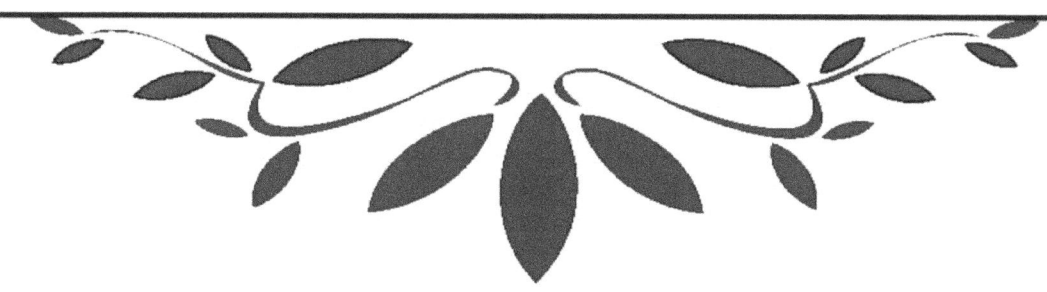

Copyright 2019 By John Boom

50 Images

Created From Real Life Photos
For You To Colour As You Please.

ISBN 978-0-359-93587-1

9 780359 935871

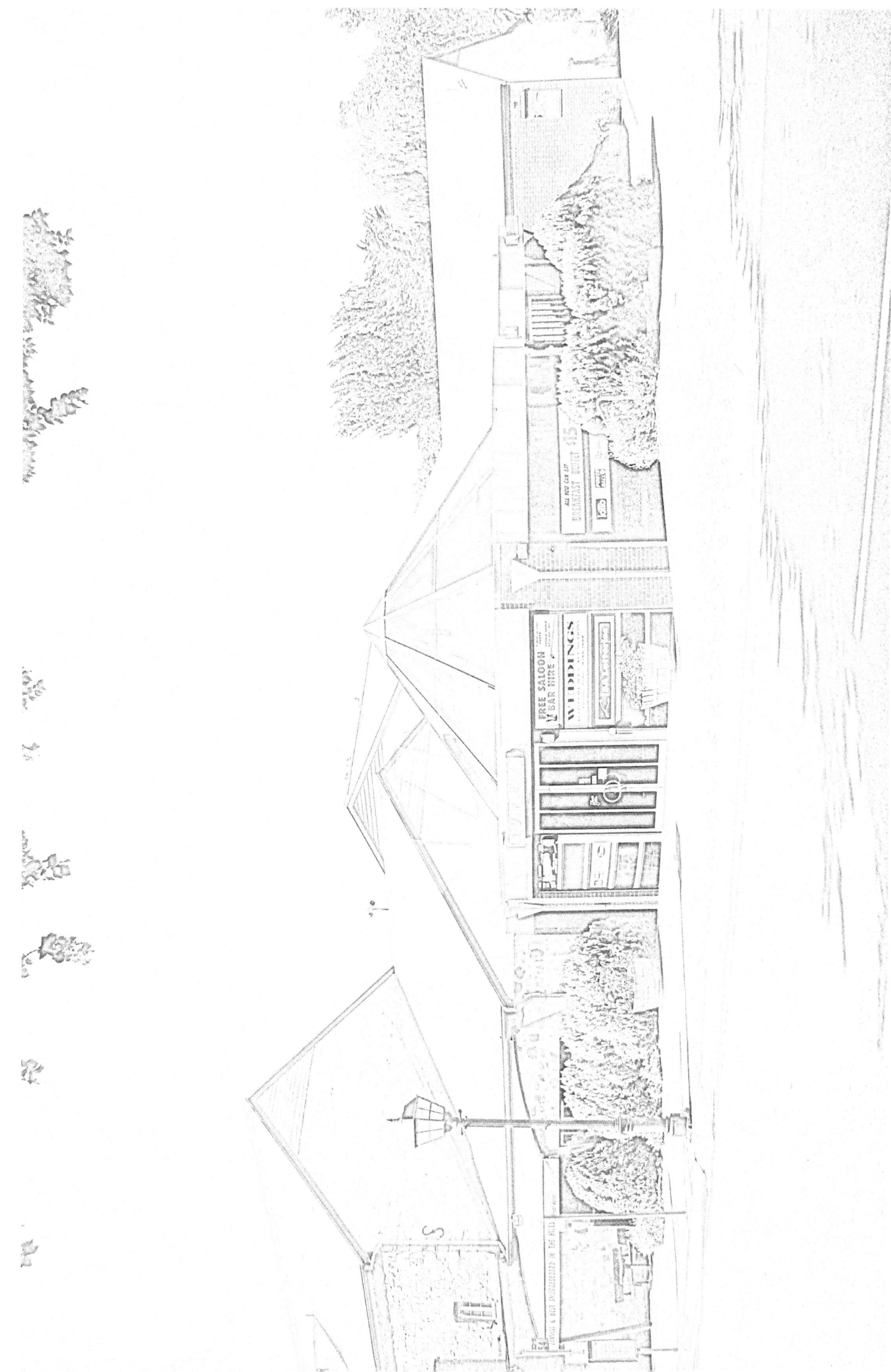

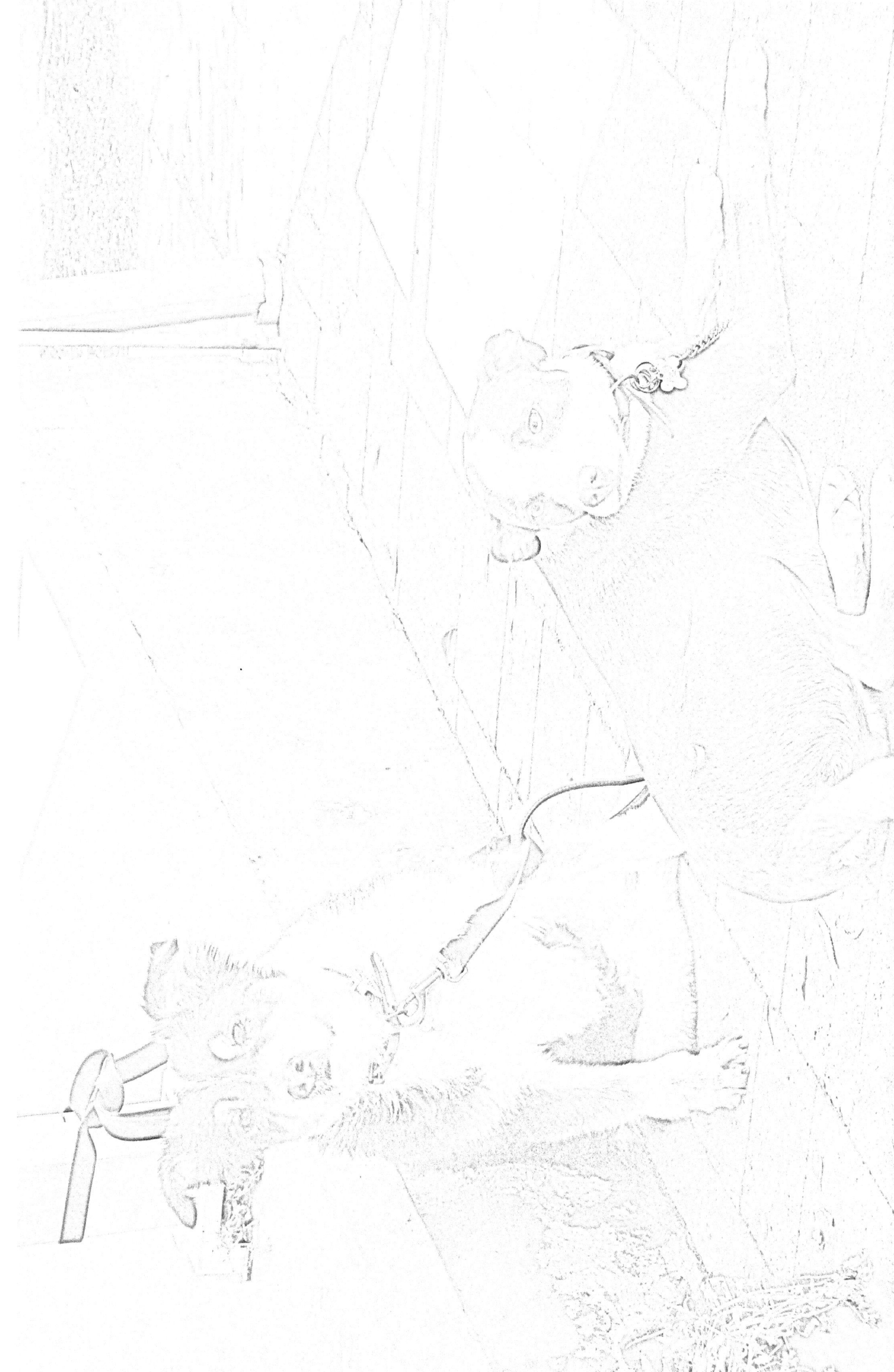

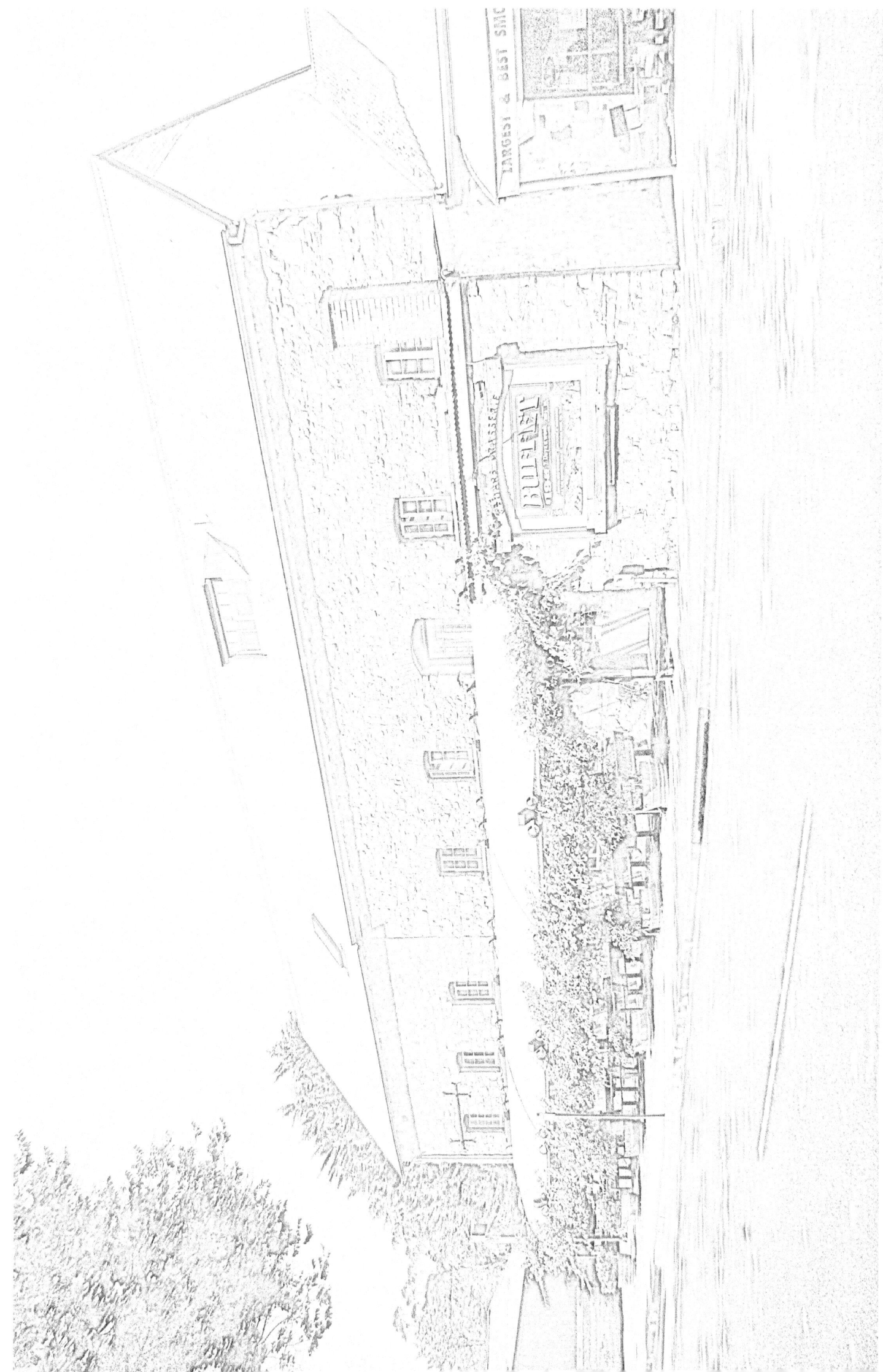

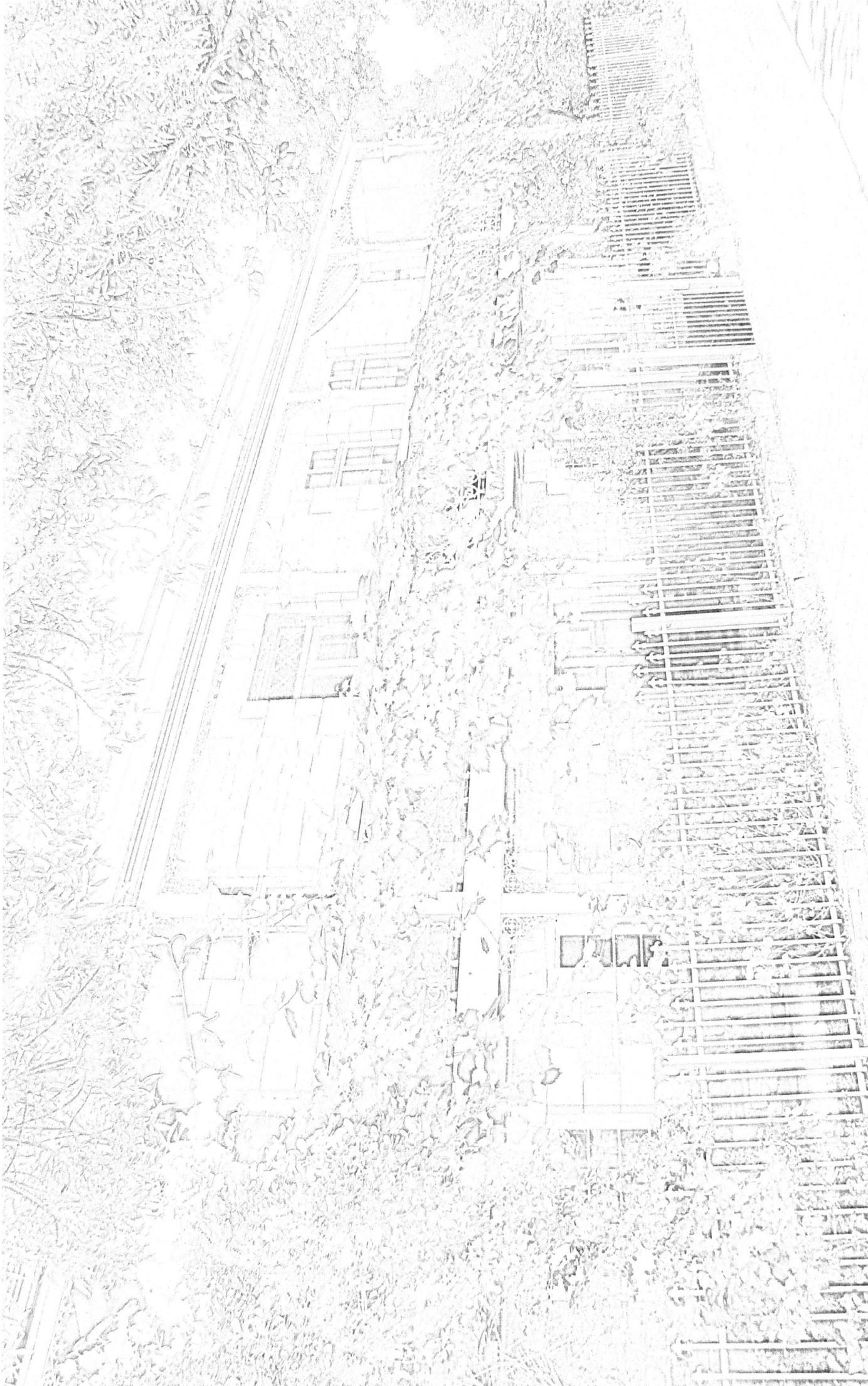

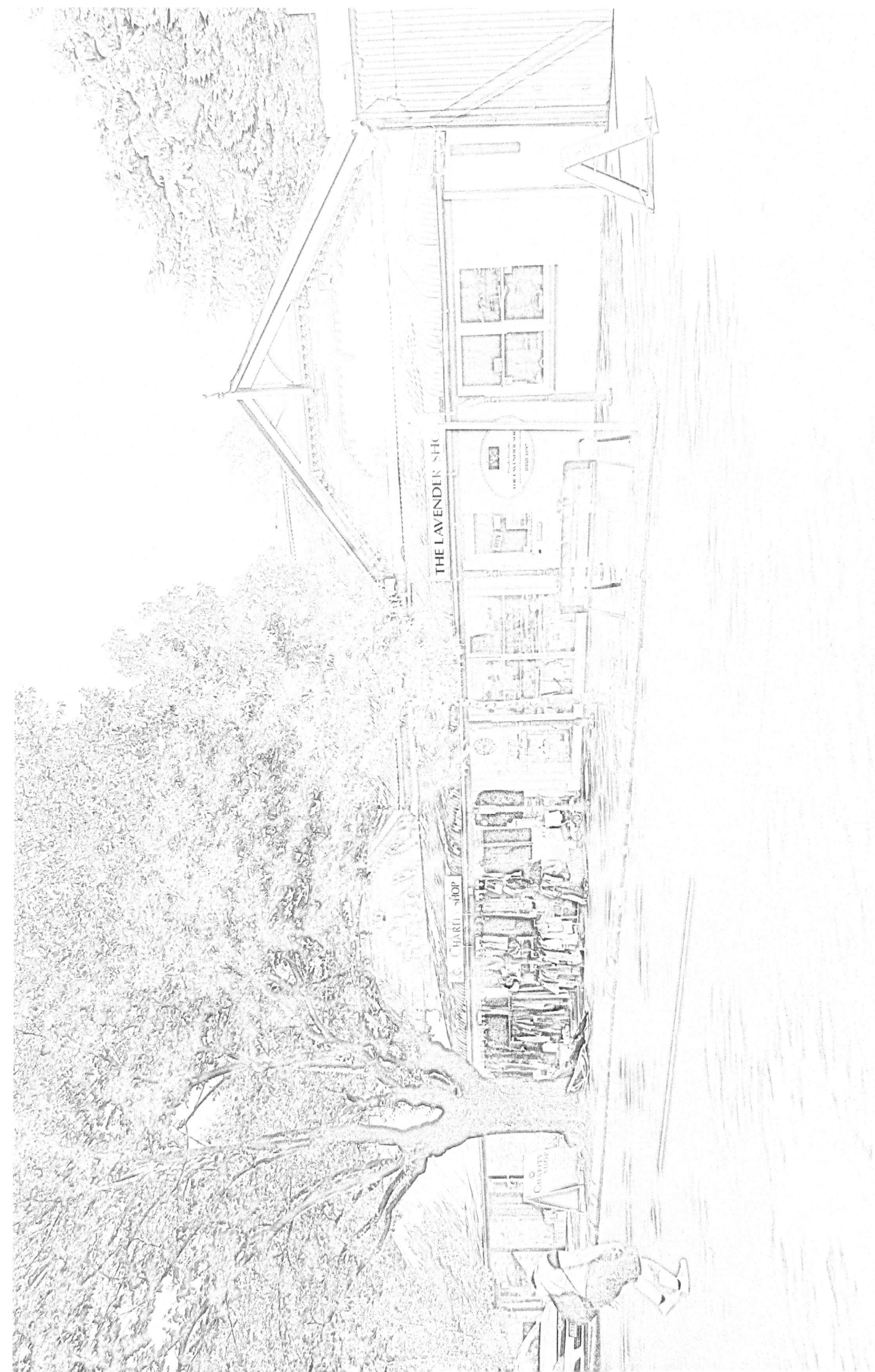

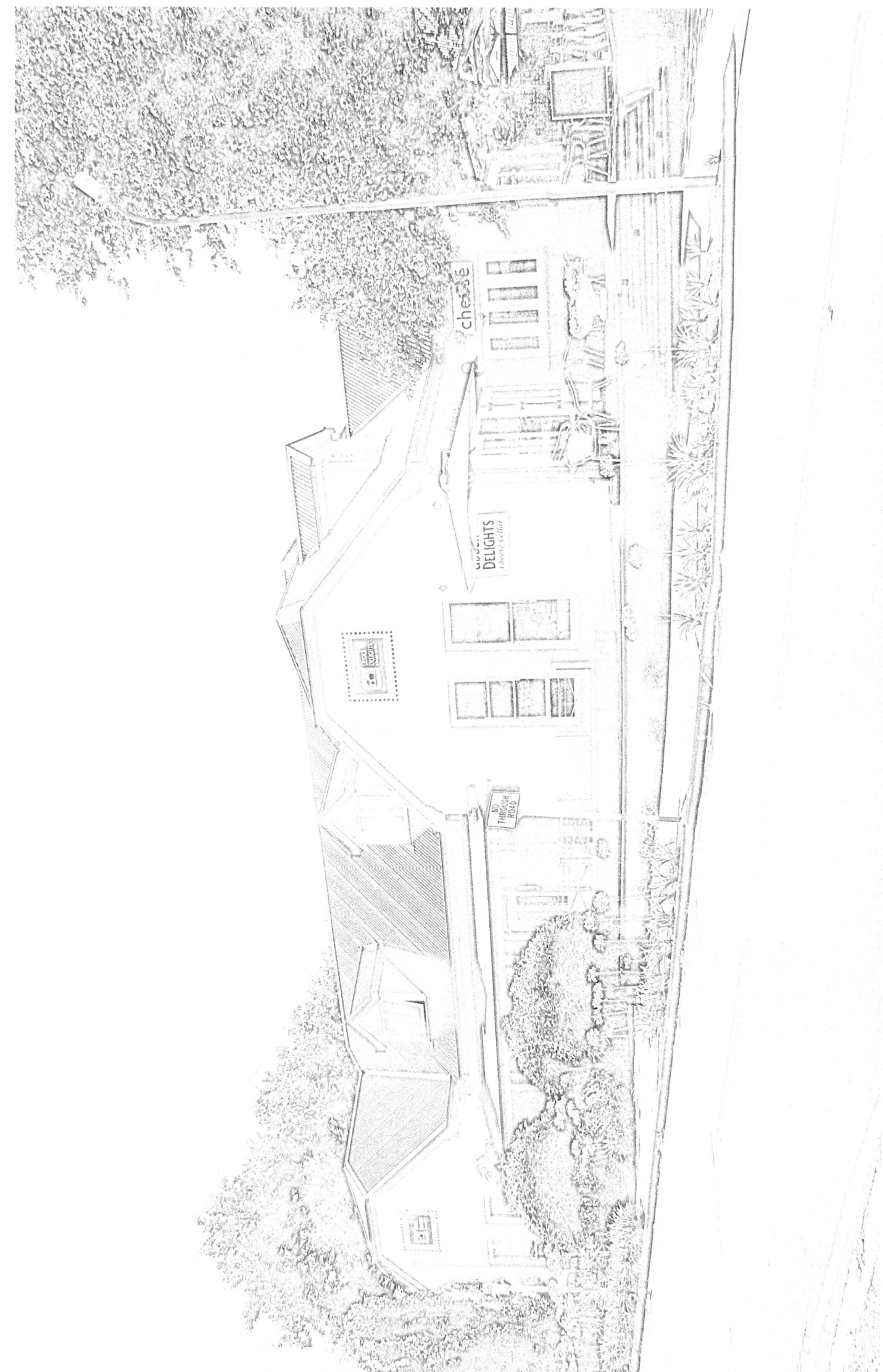

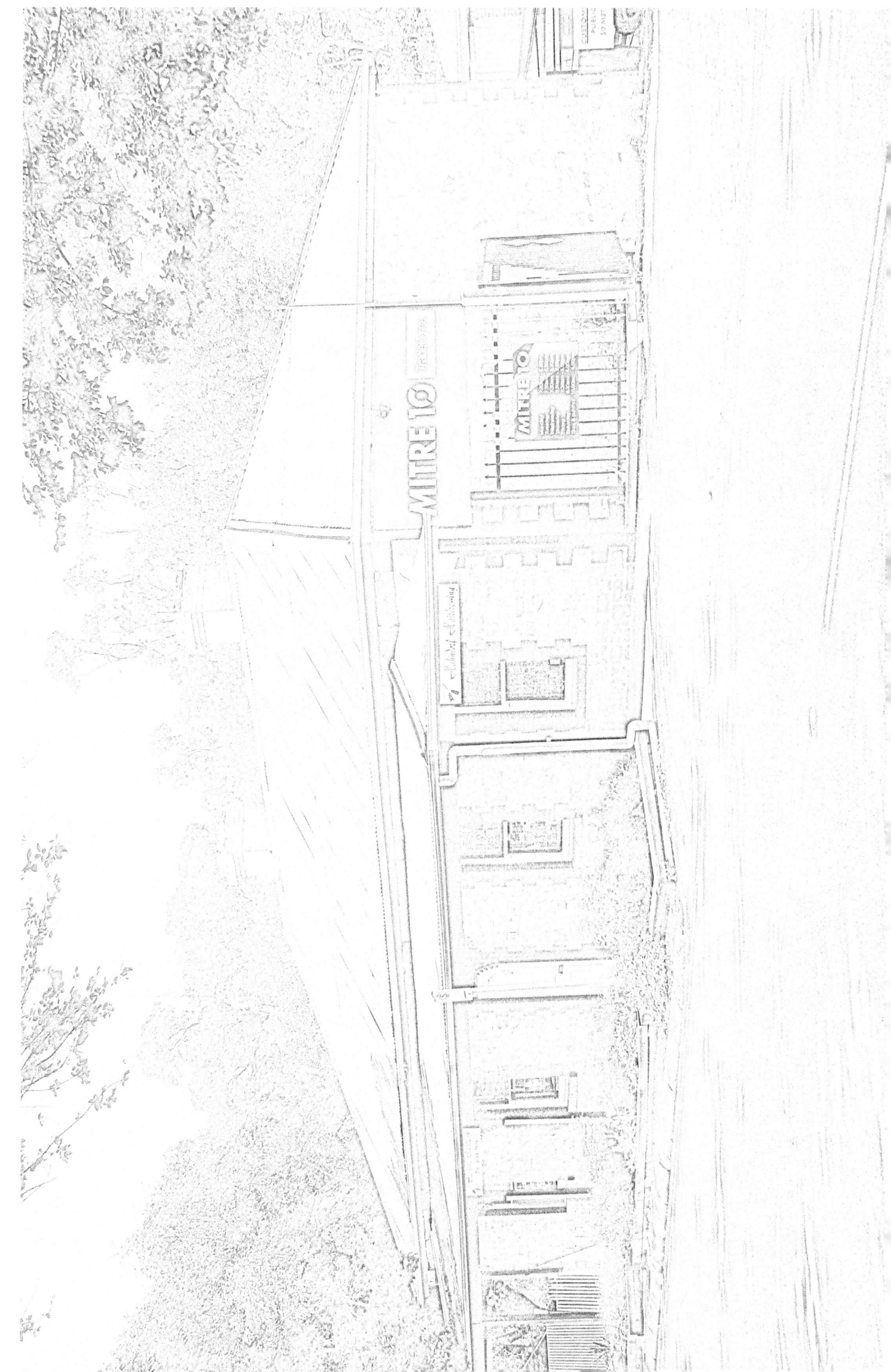

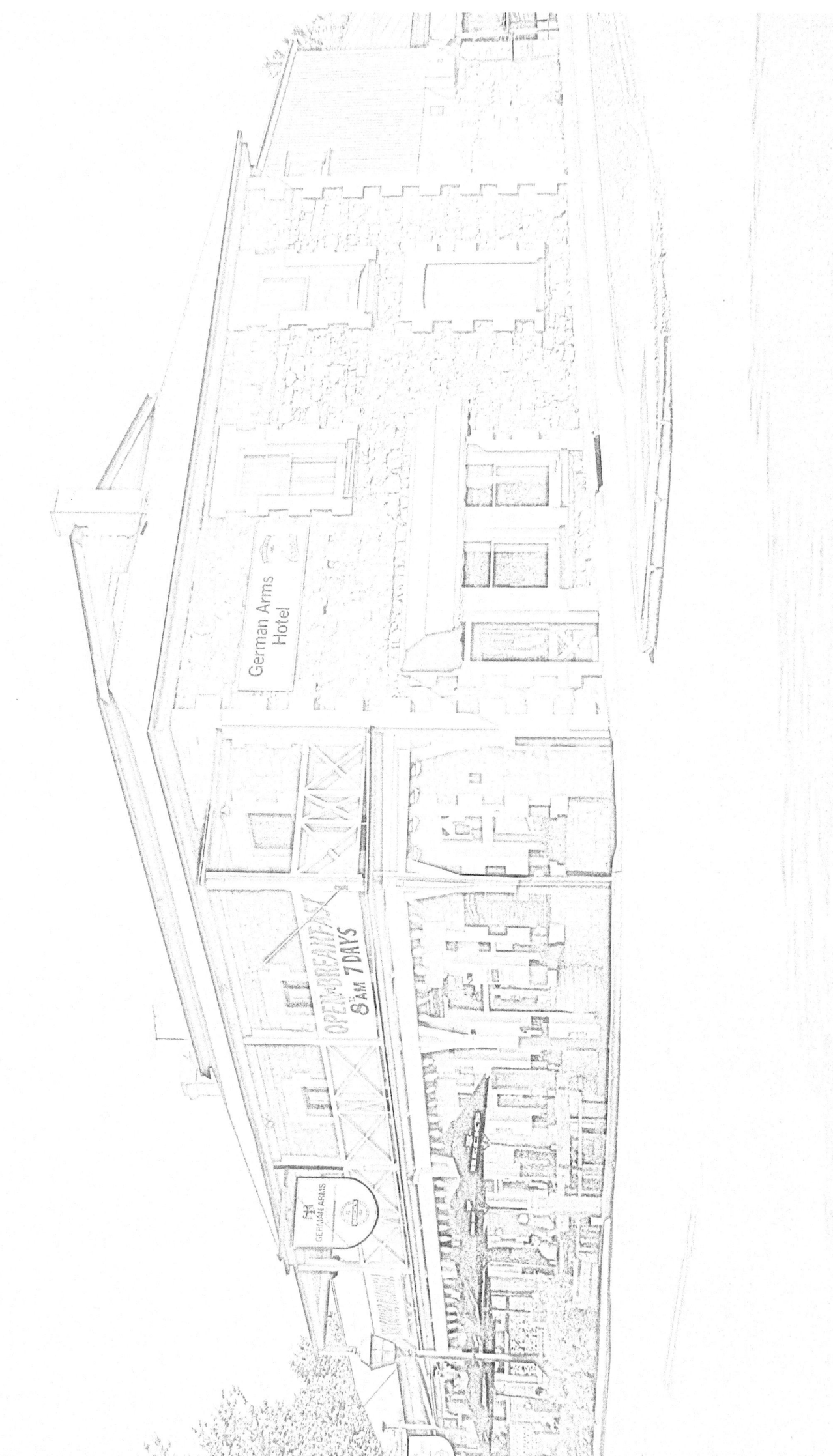

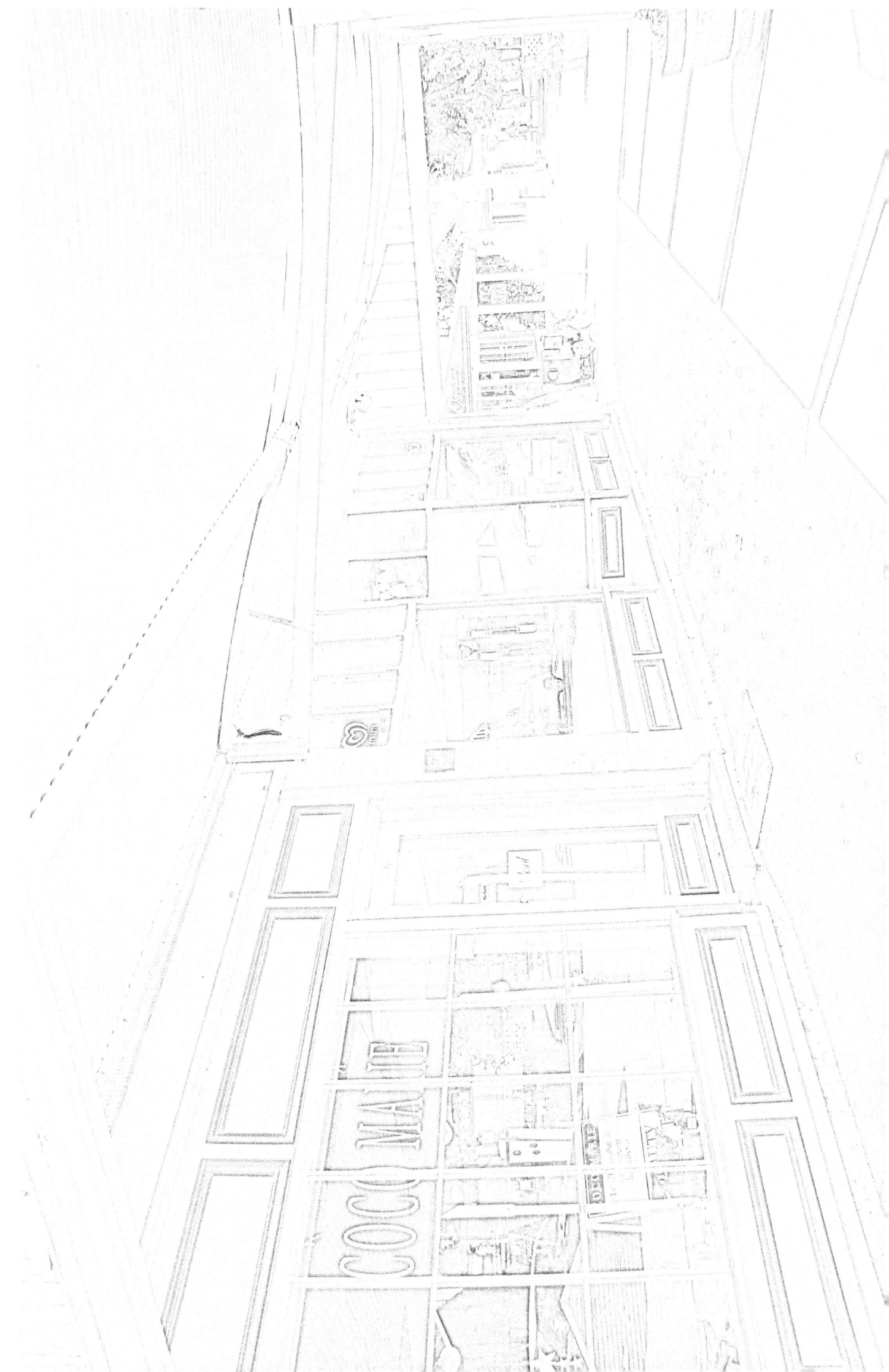

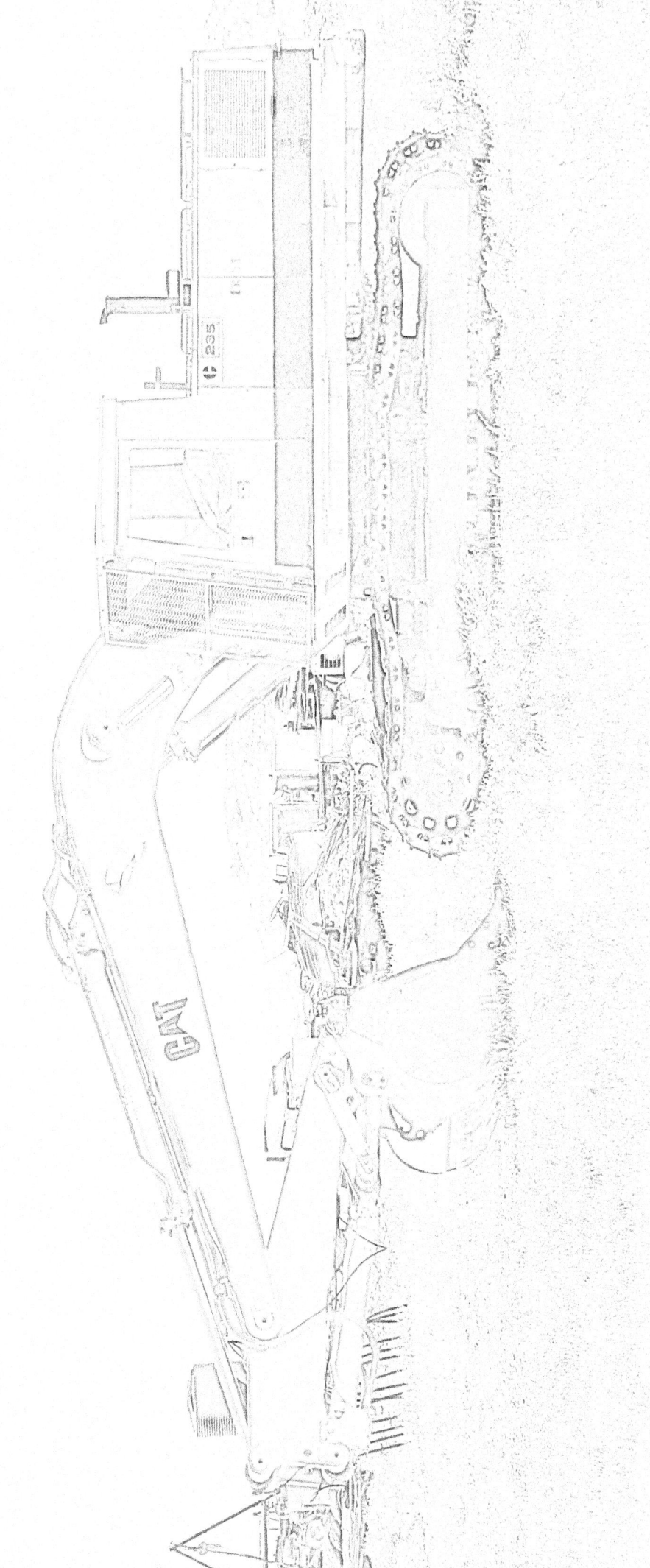

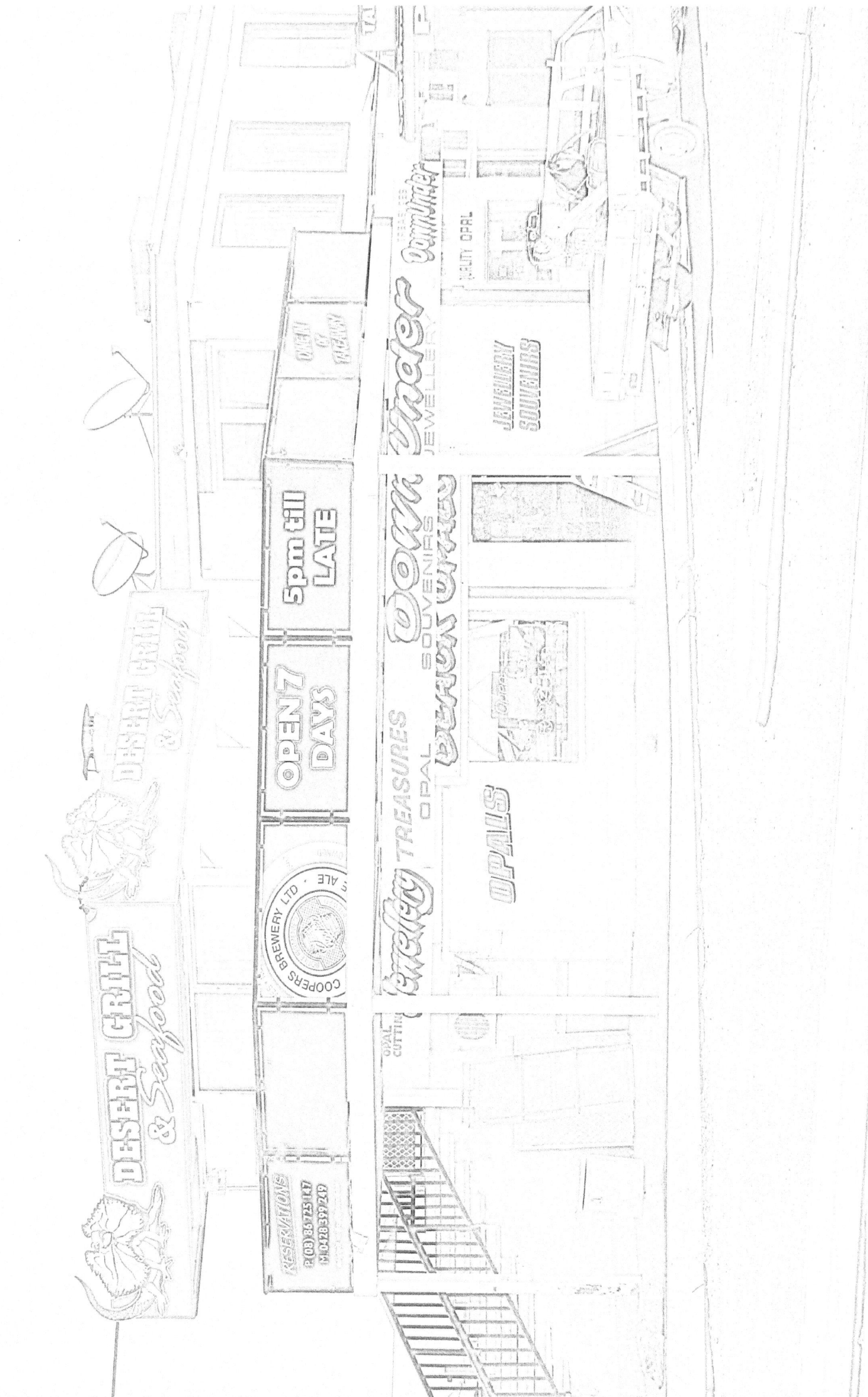

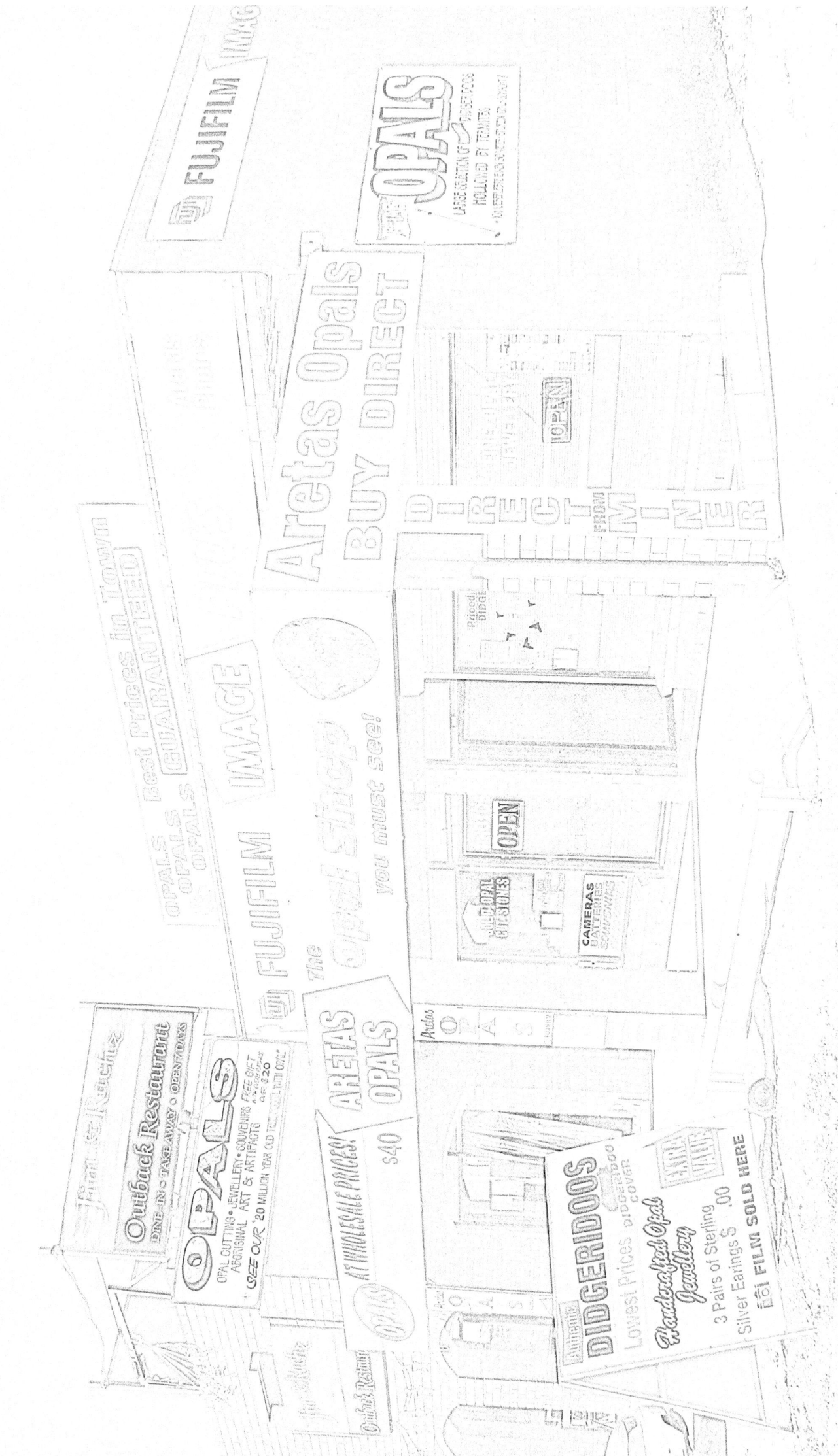

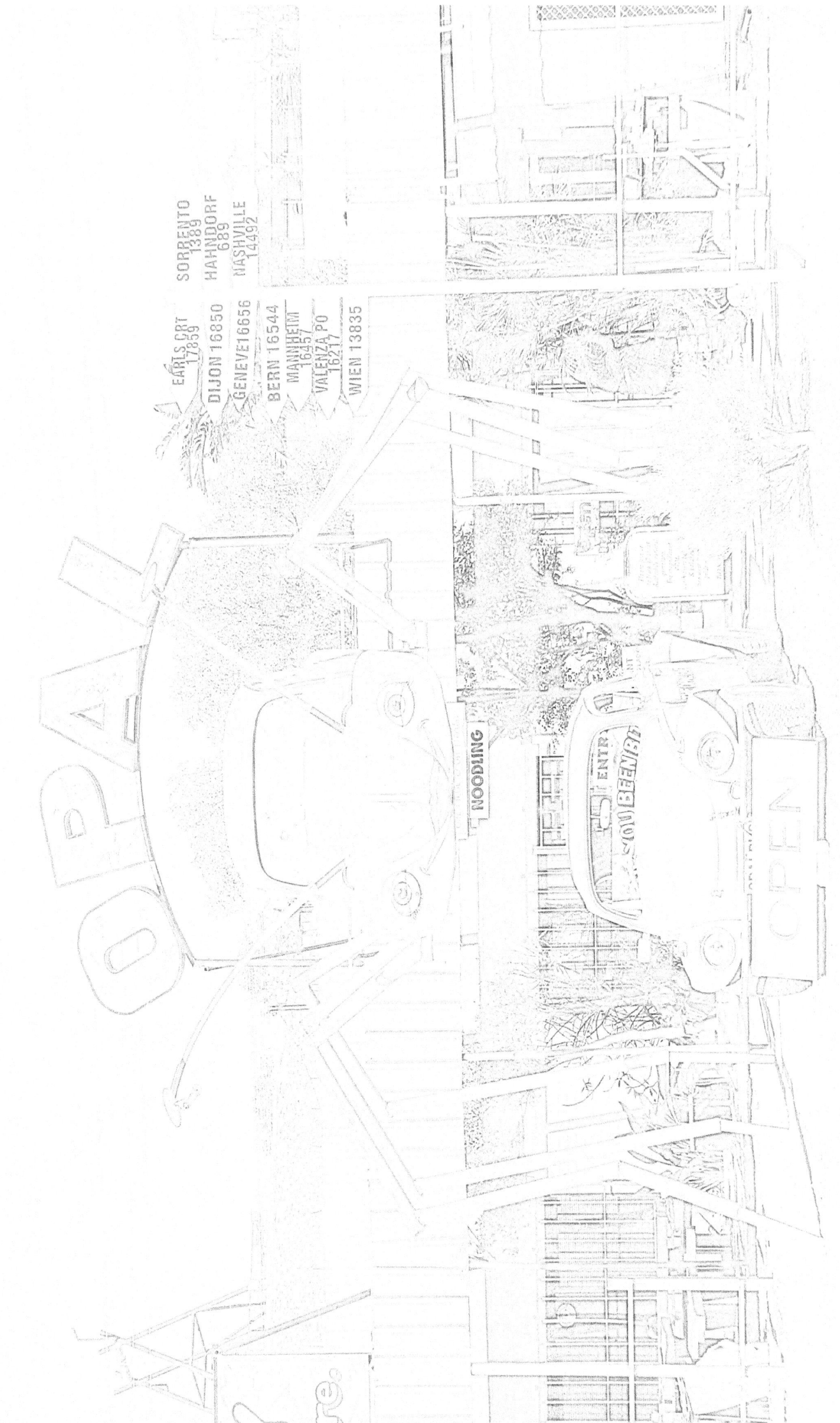

This wagon travelled with supplies from Adelaide to Anna Creek Station in 1875

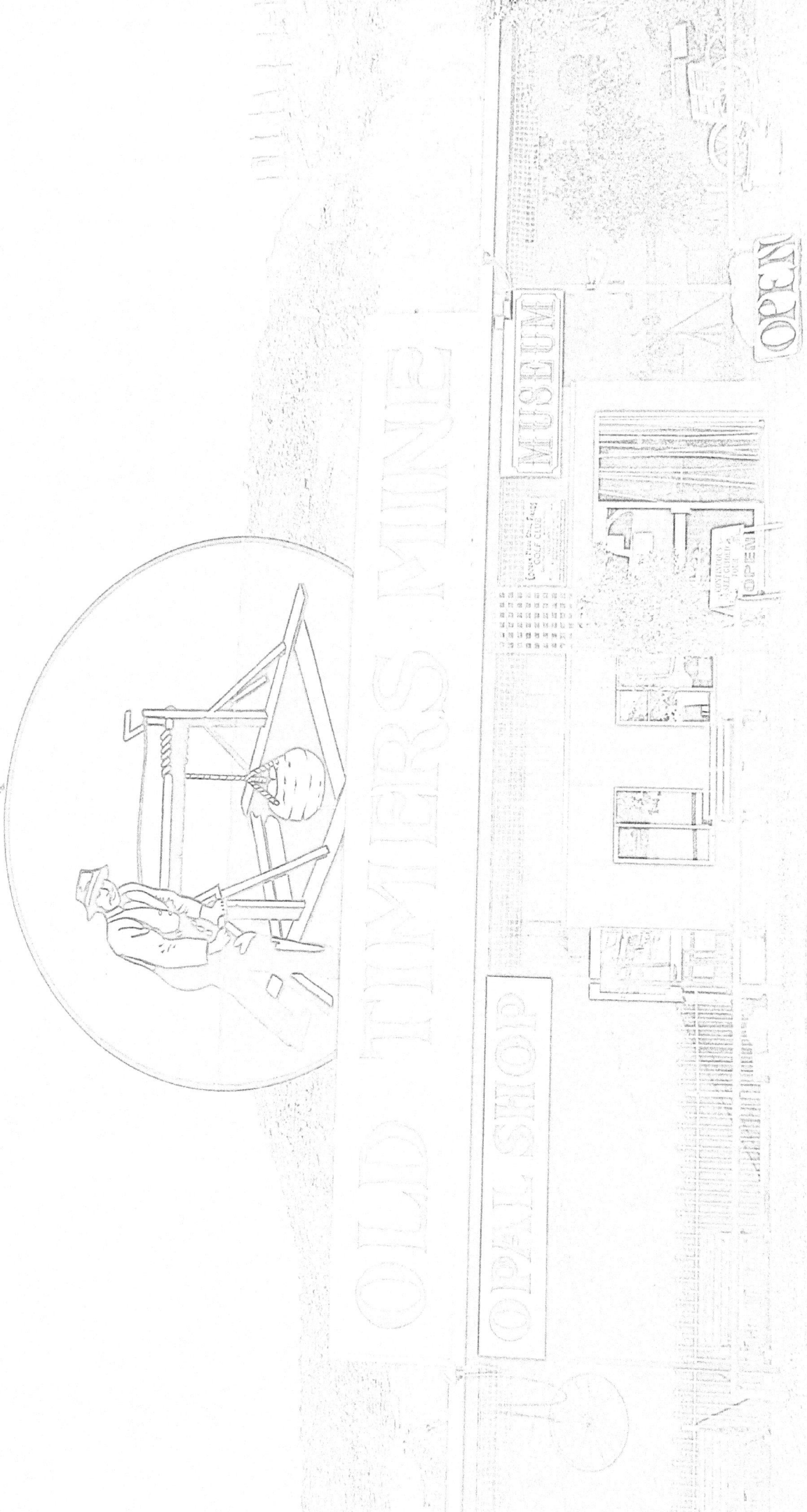

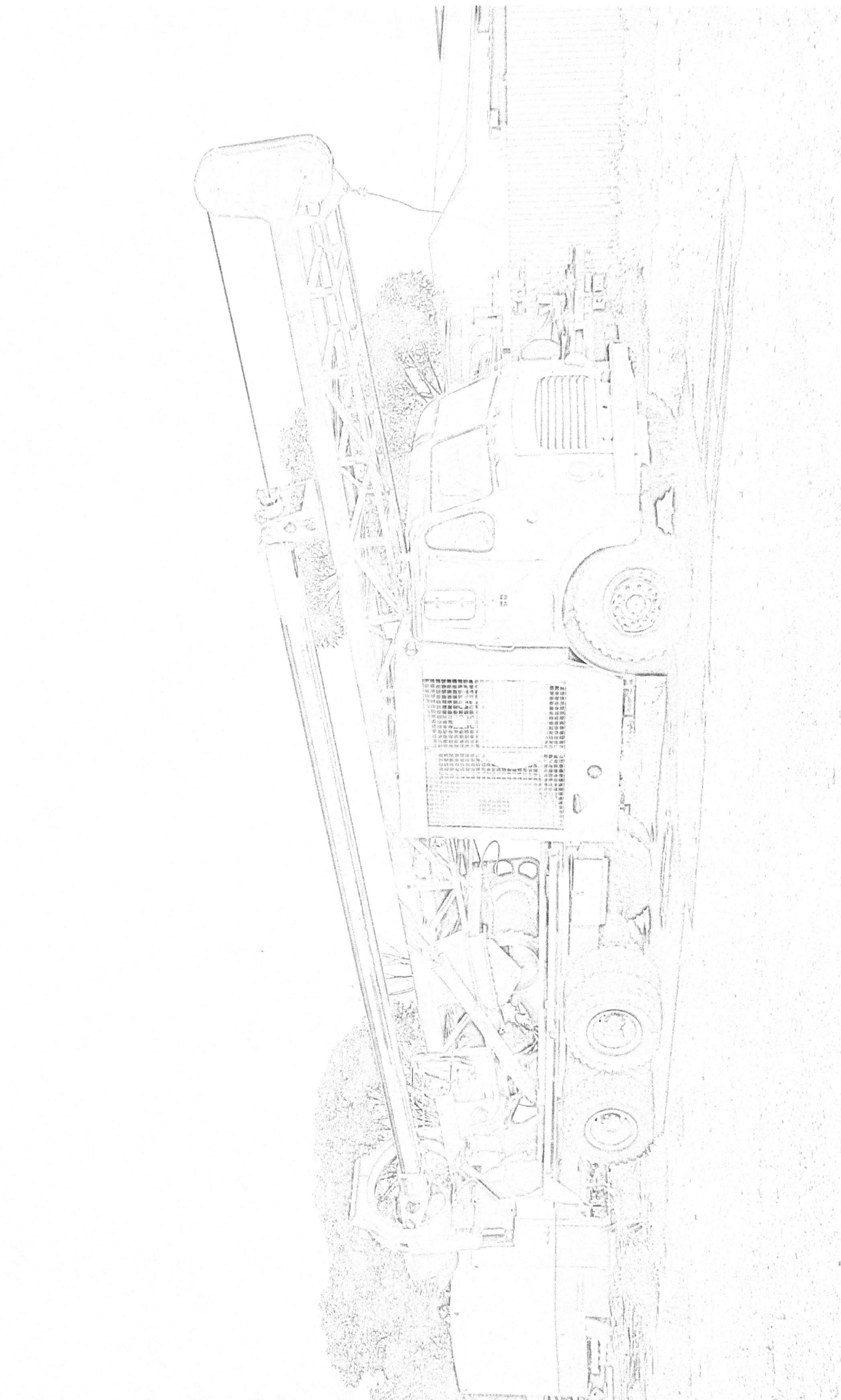

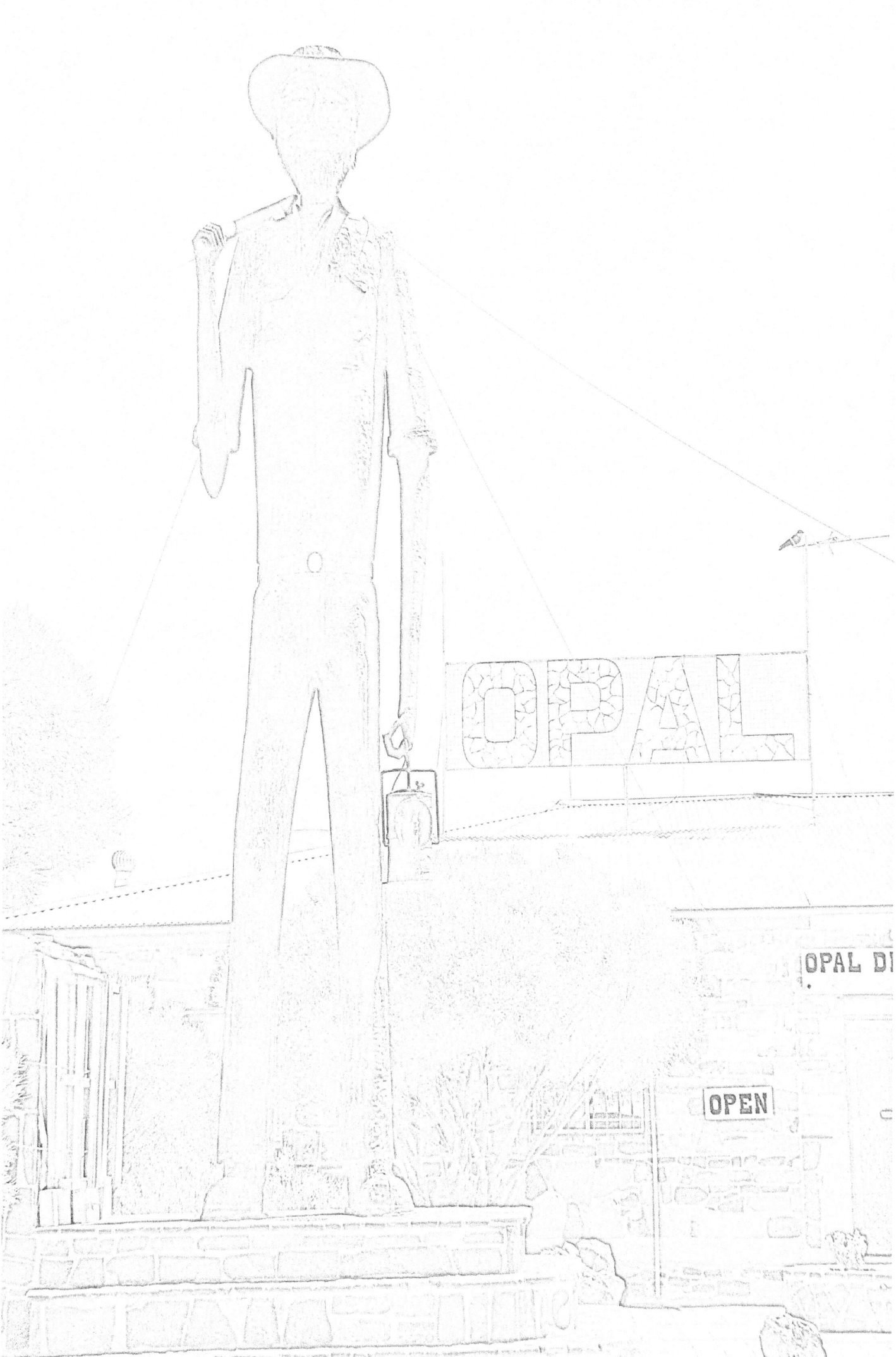

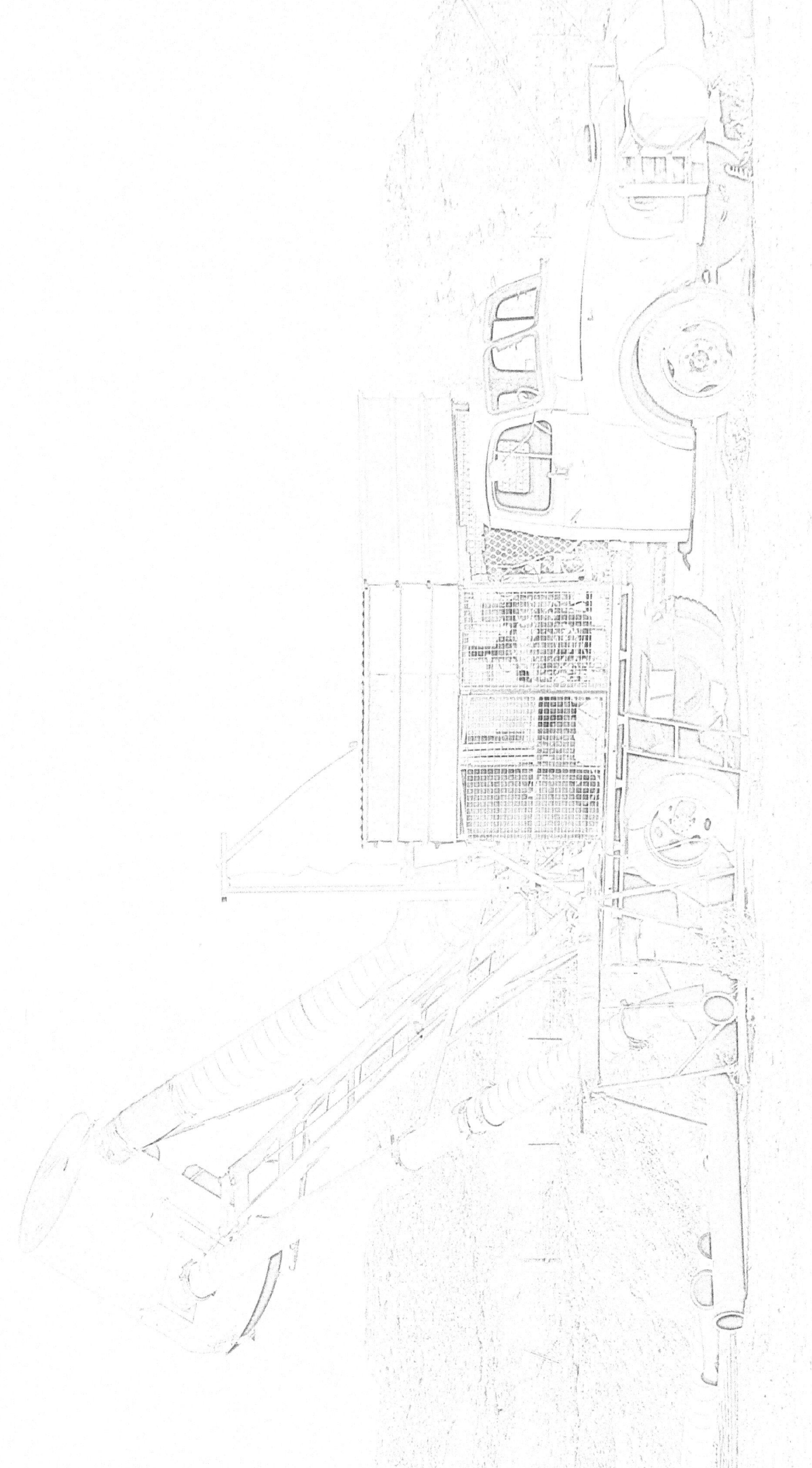

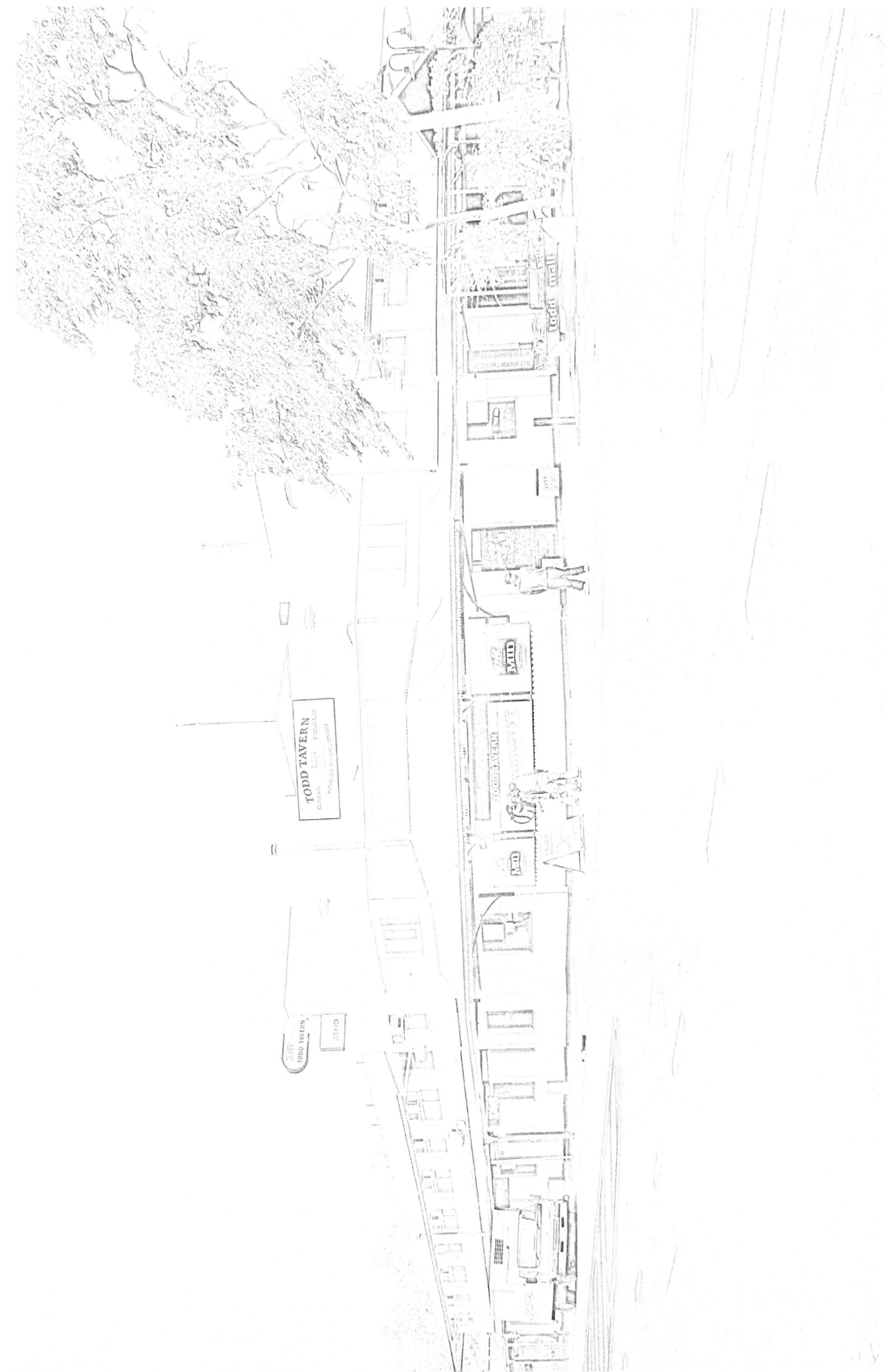

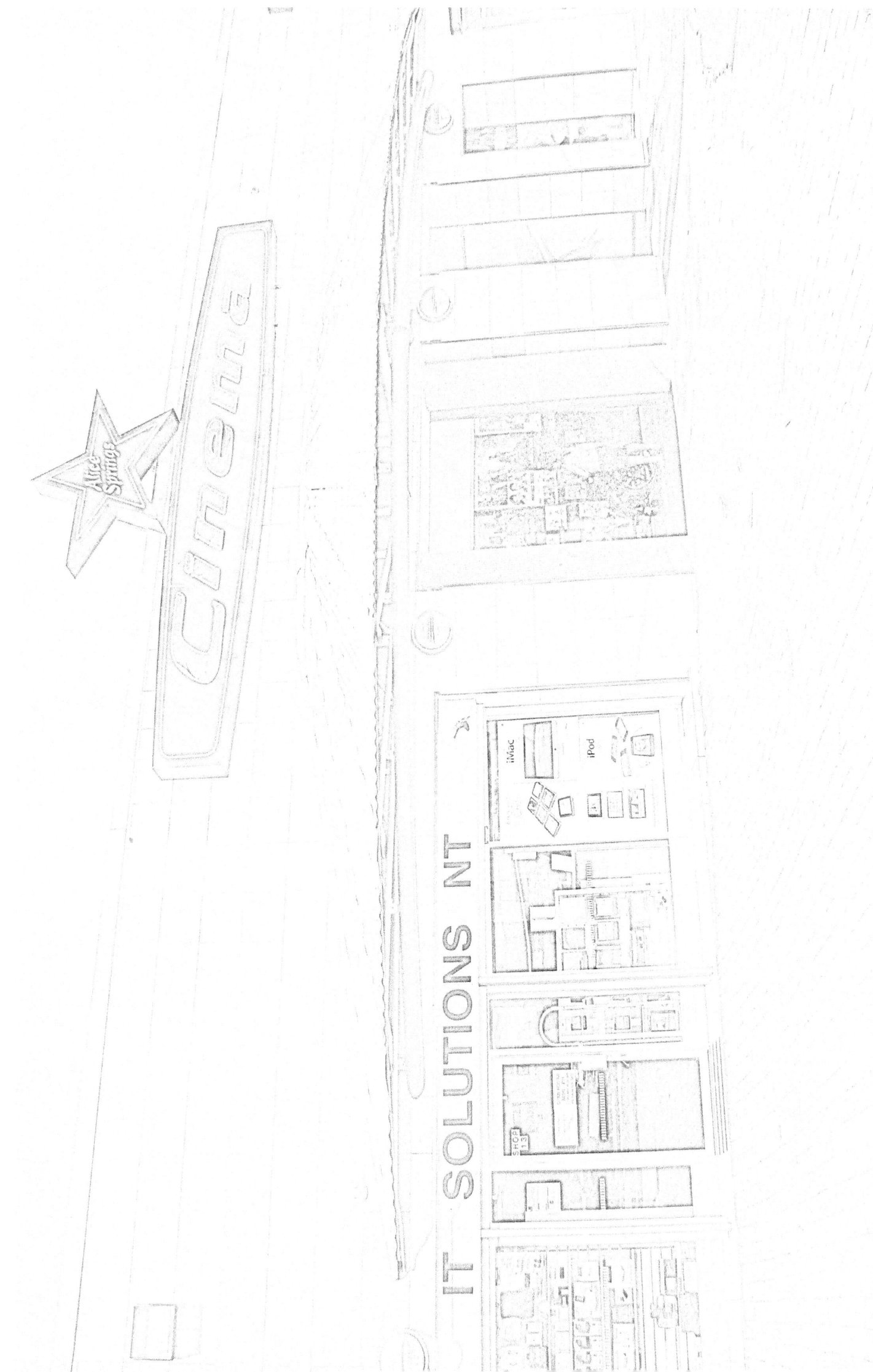

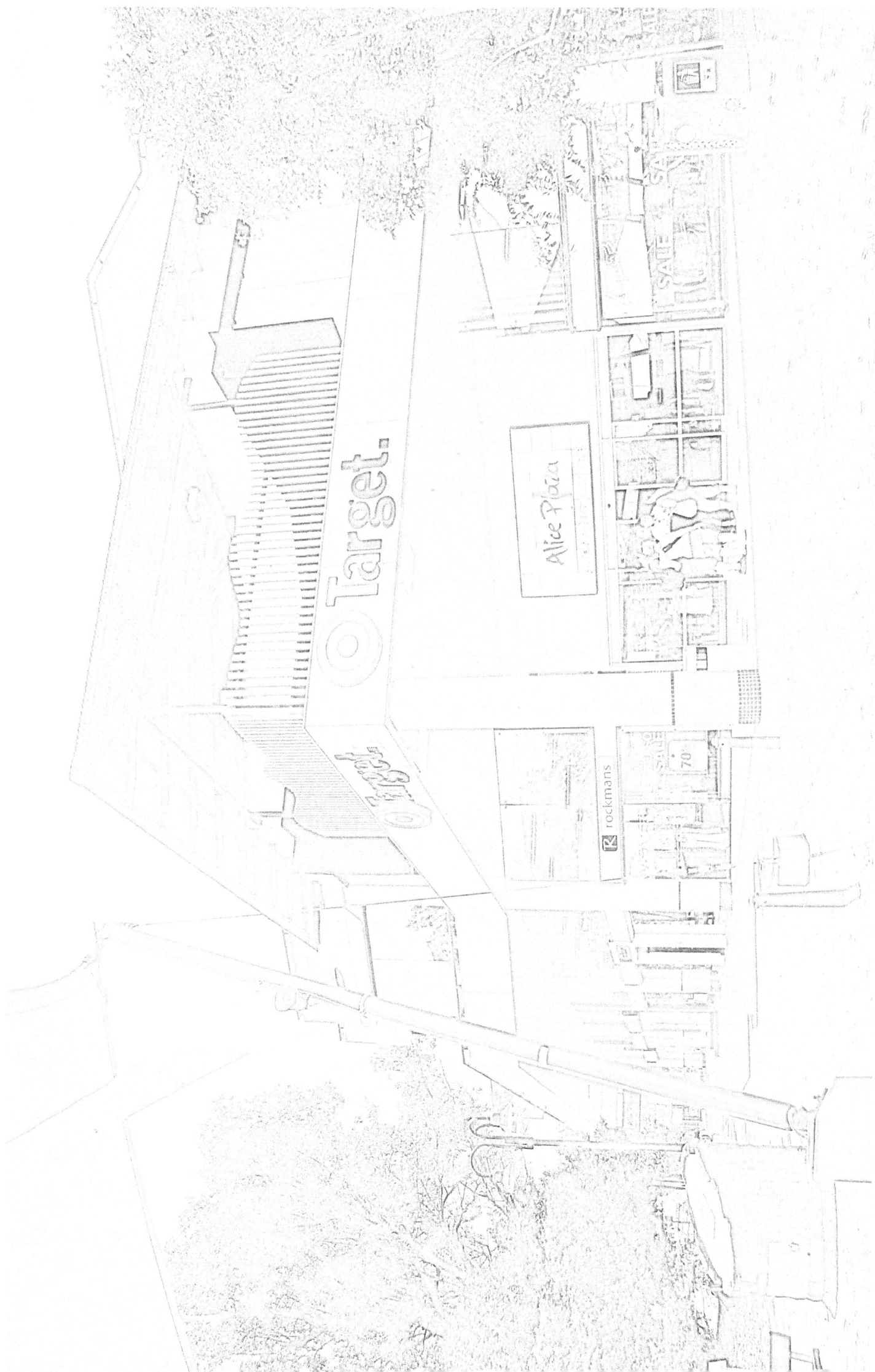

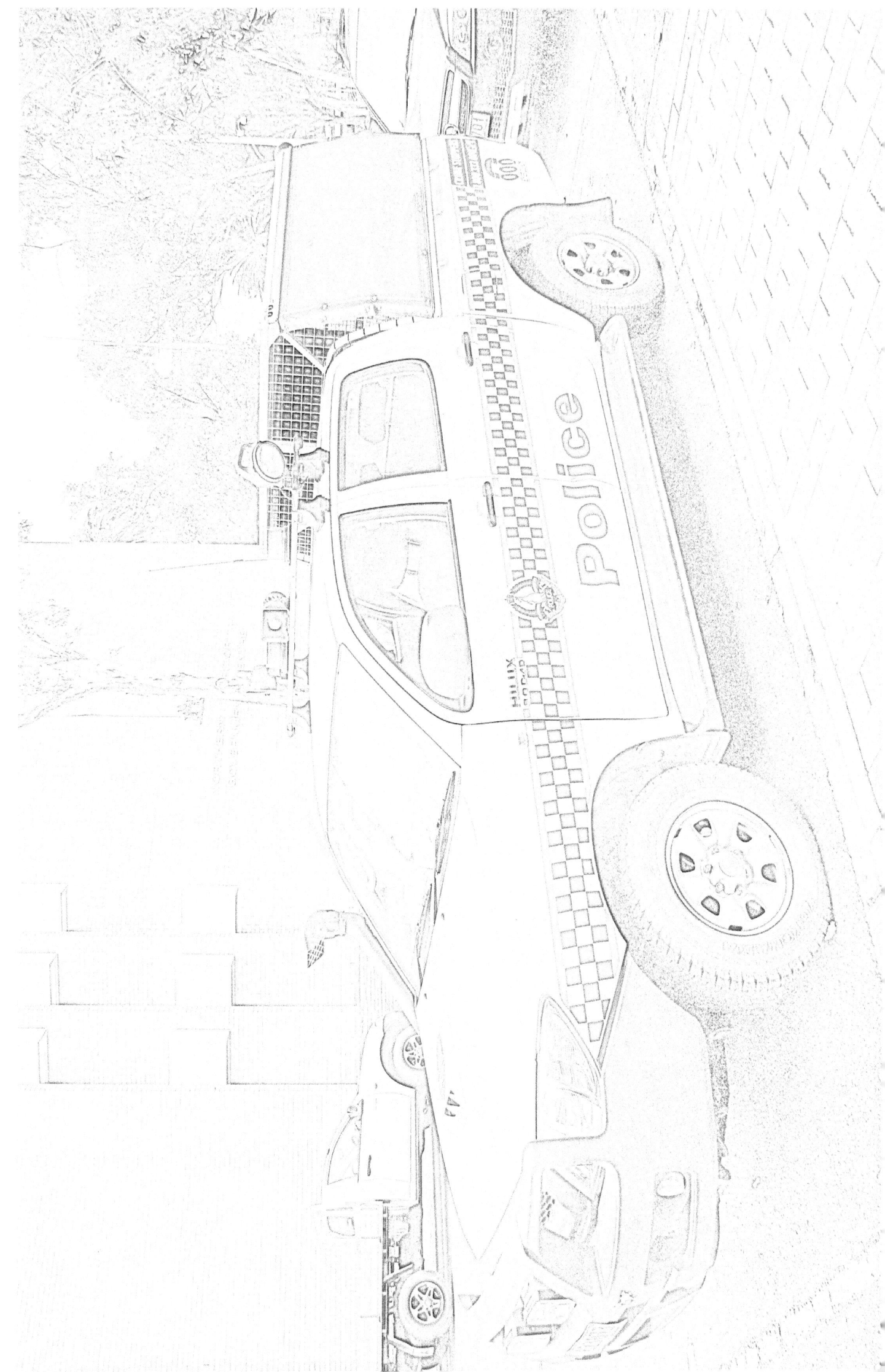

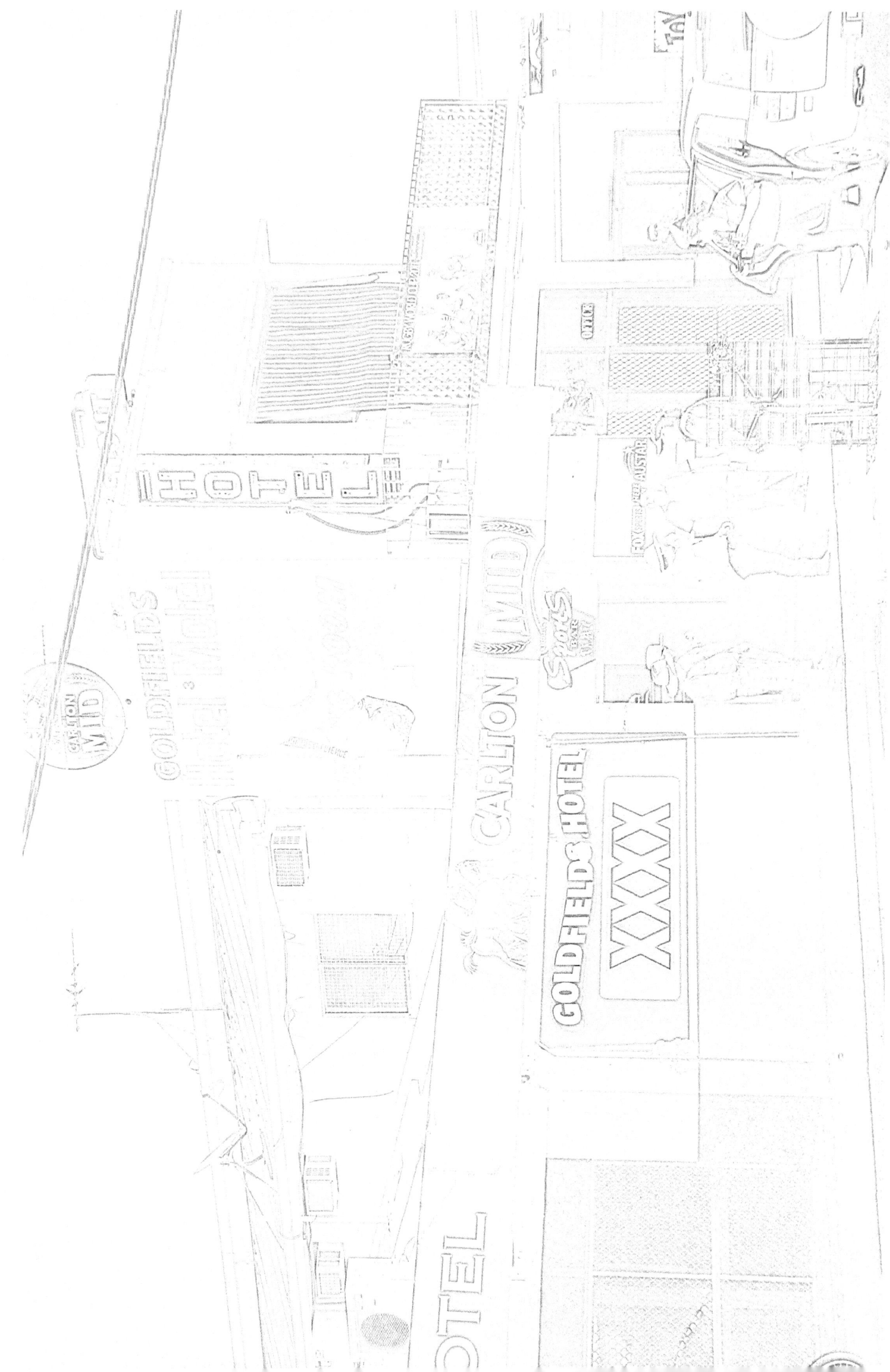

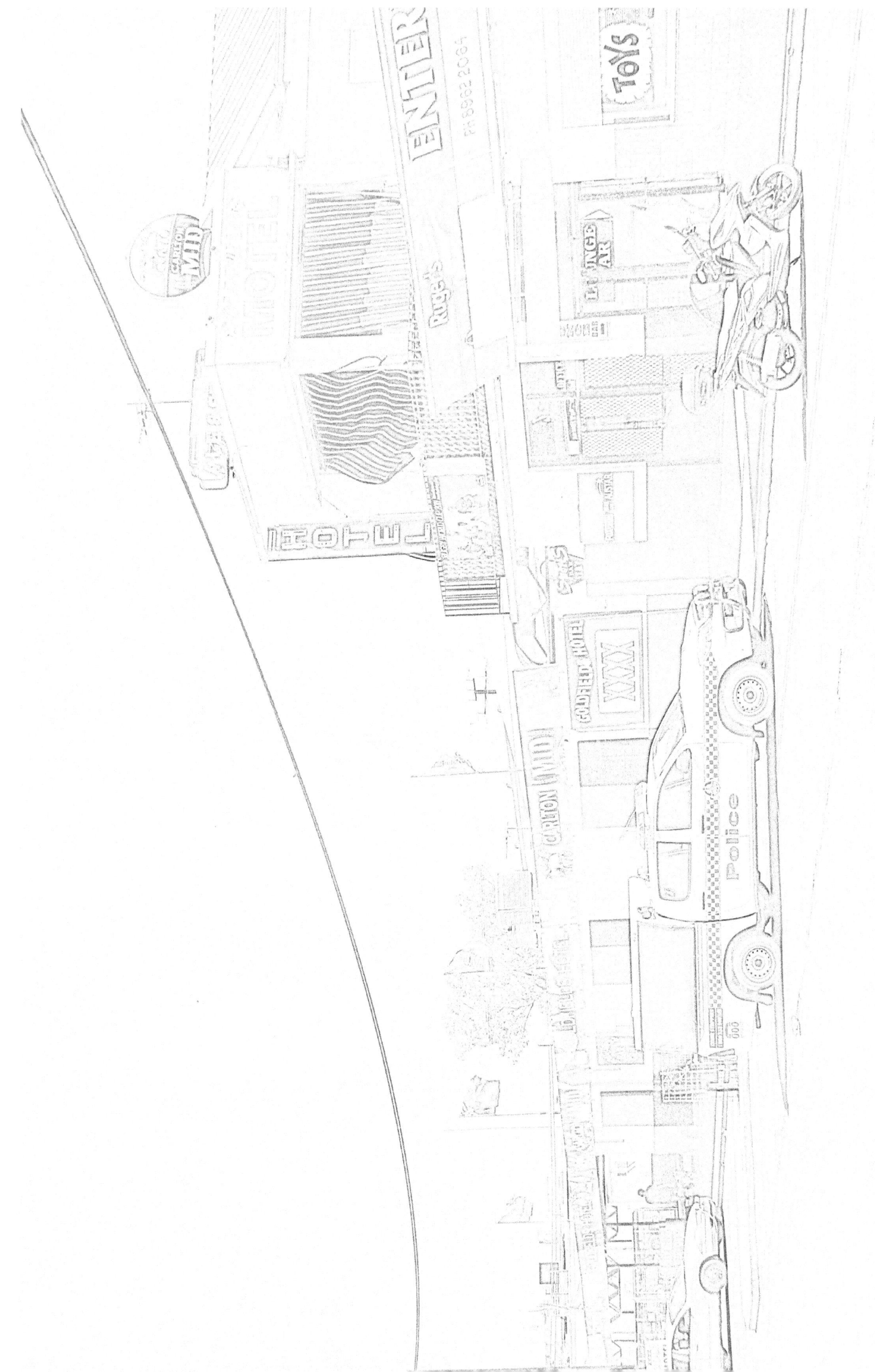

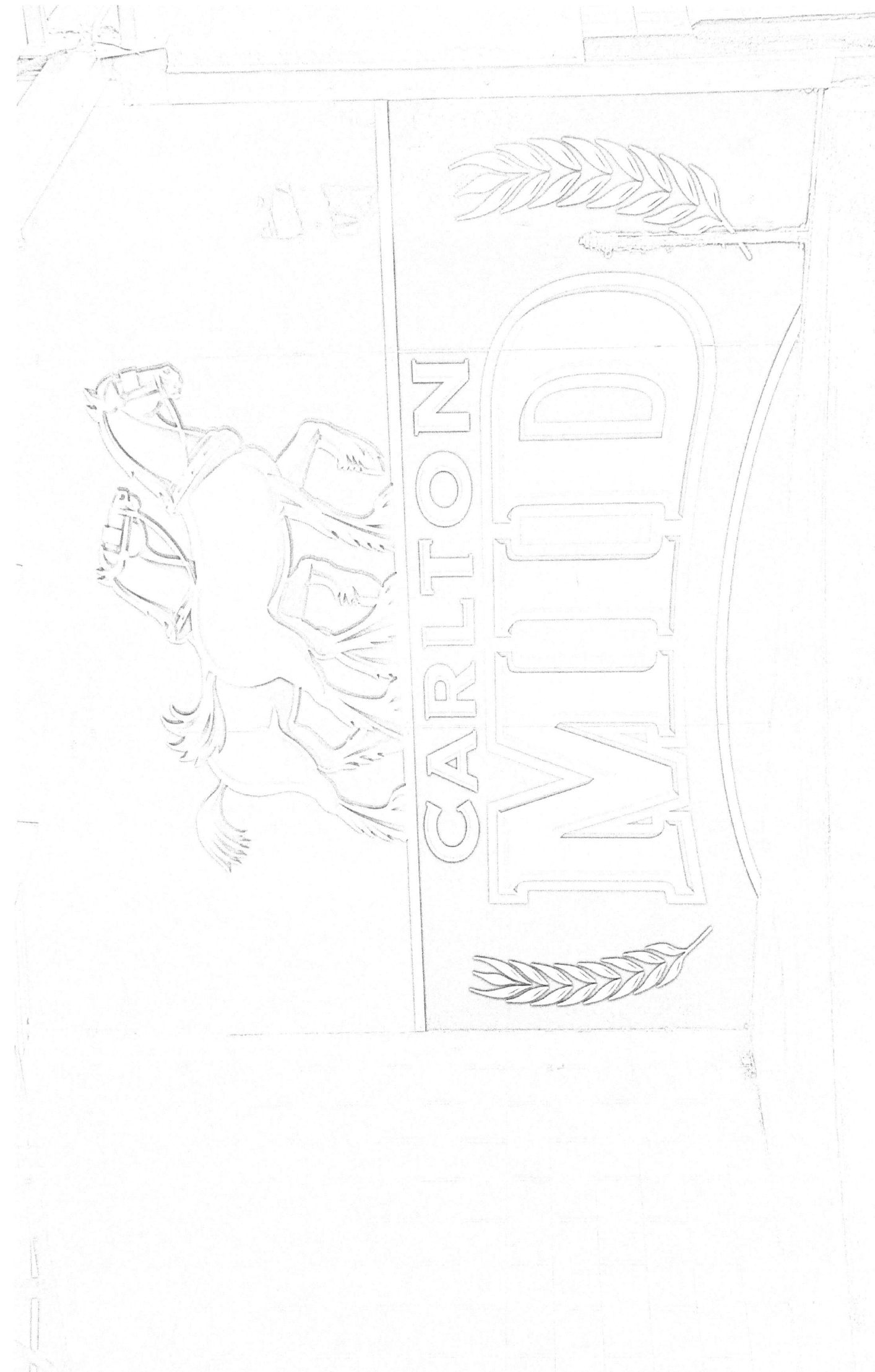

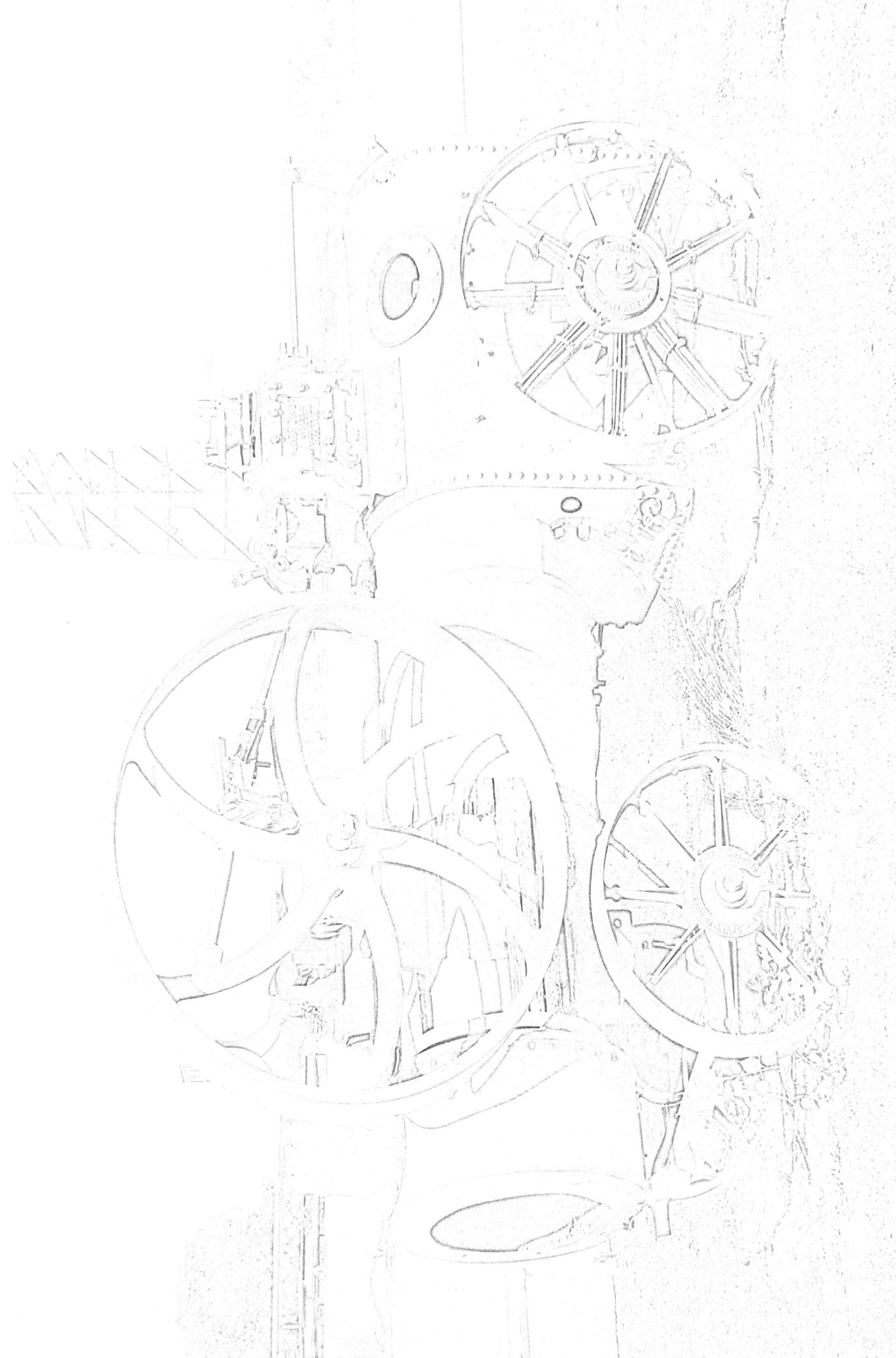

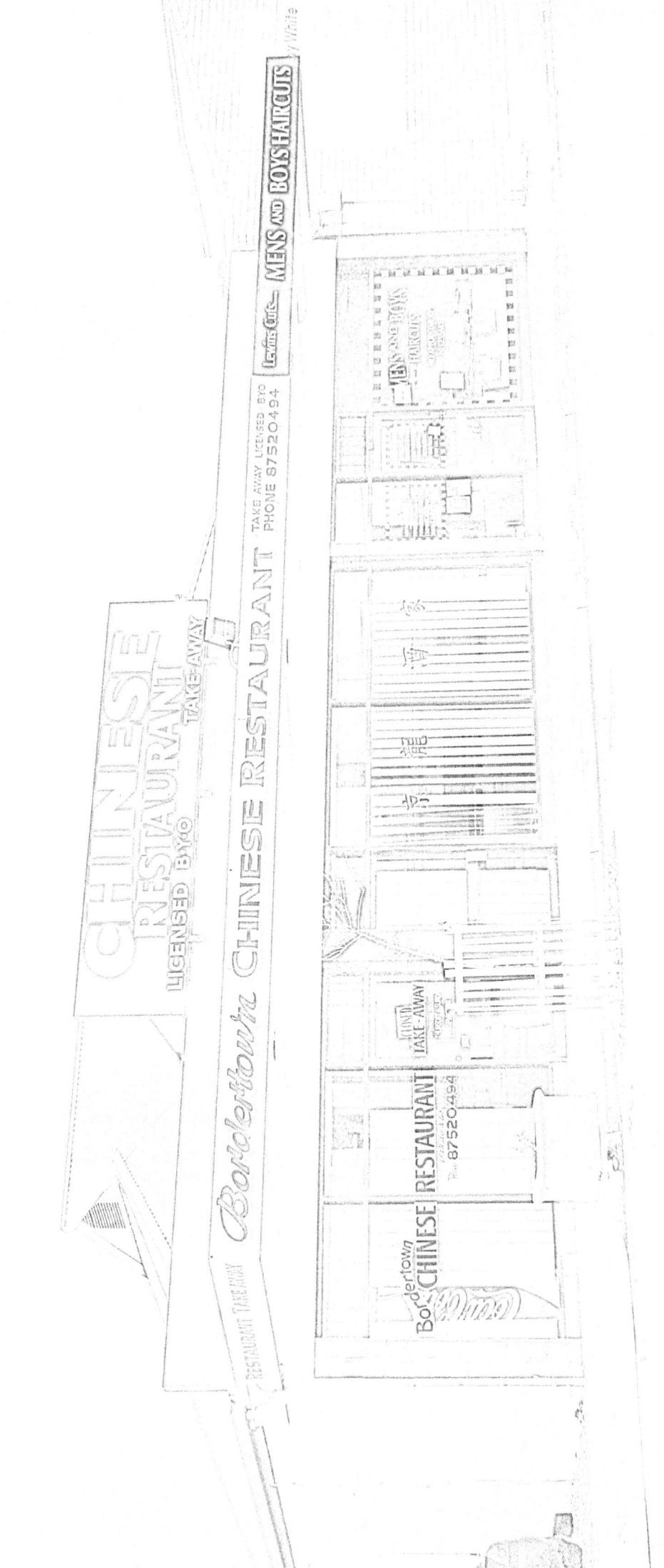

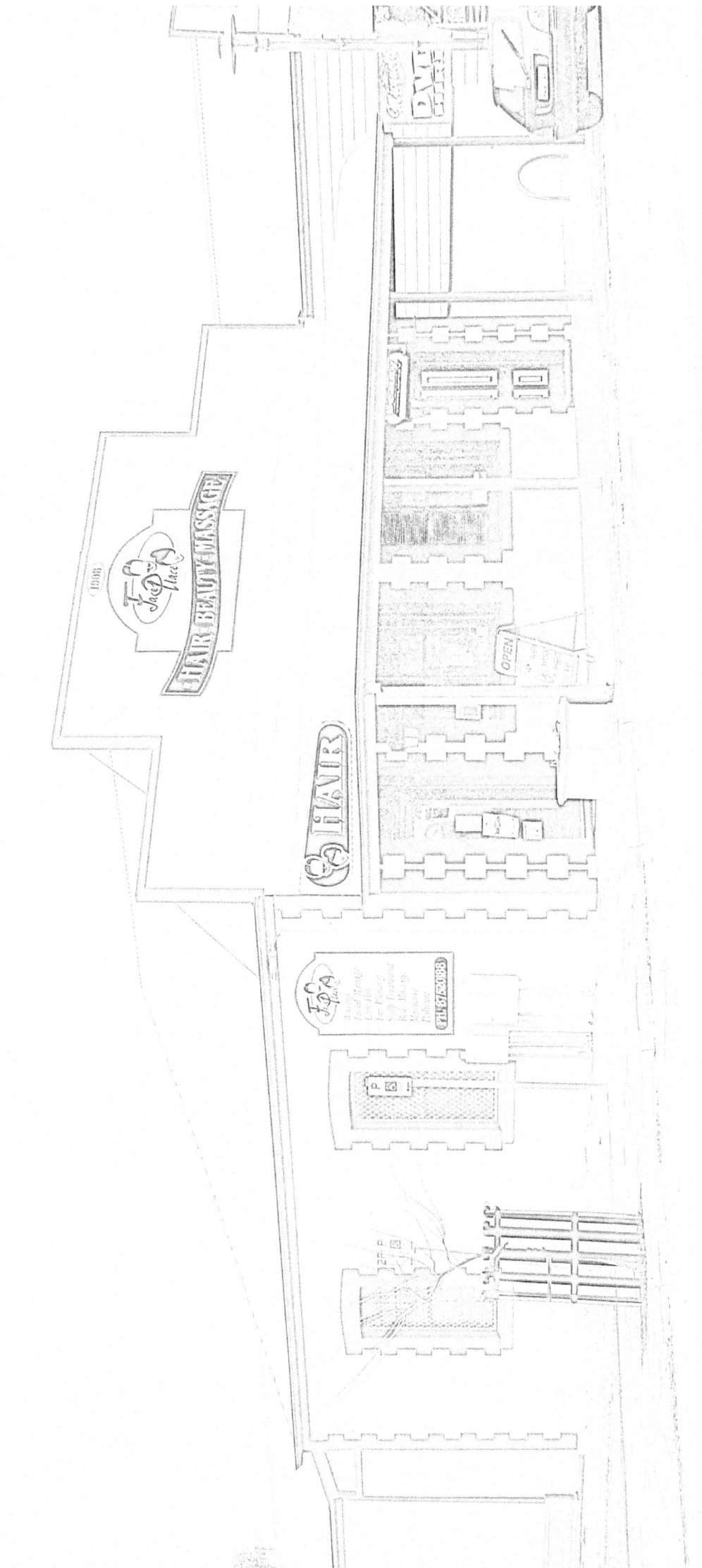

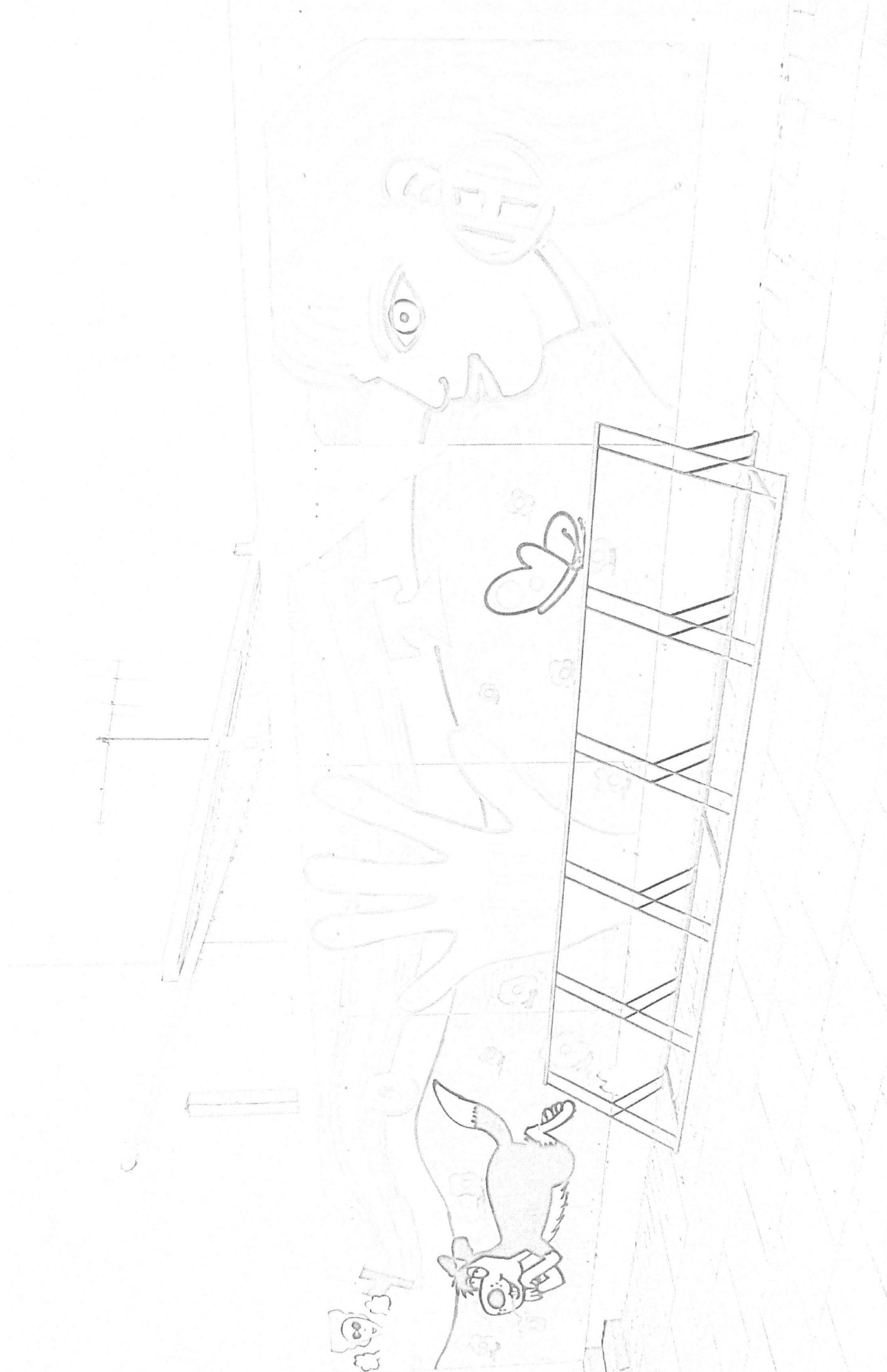

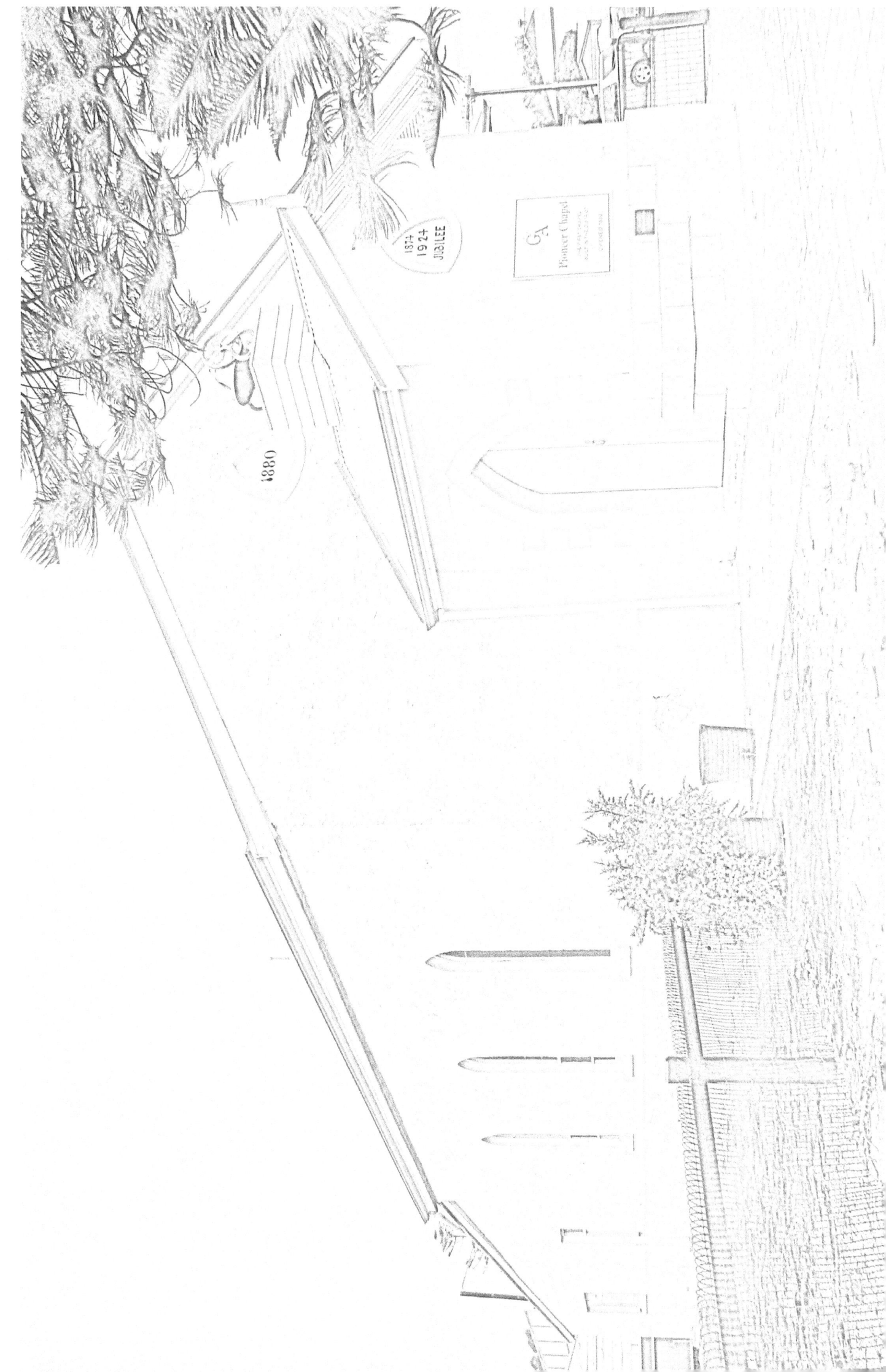

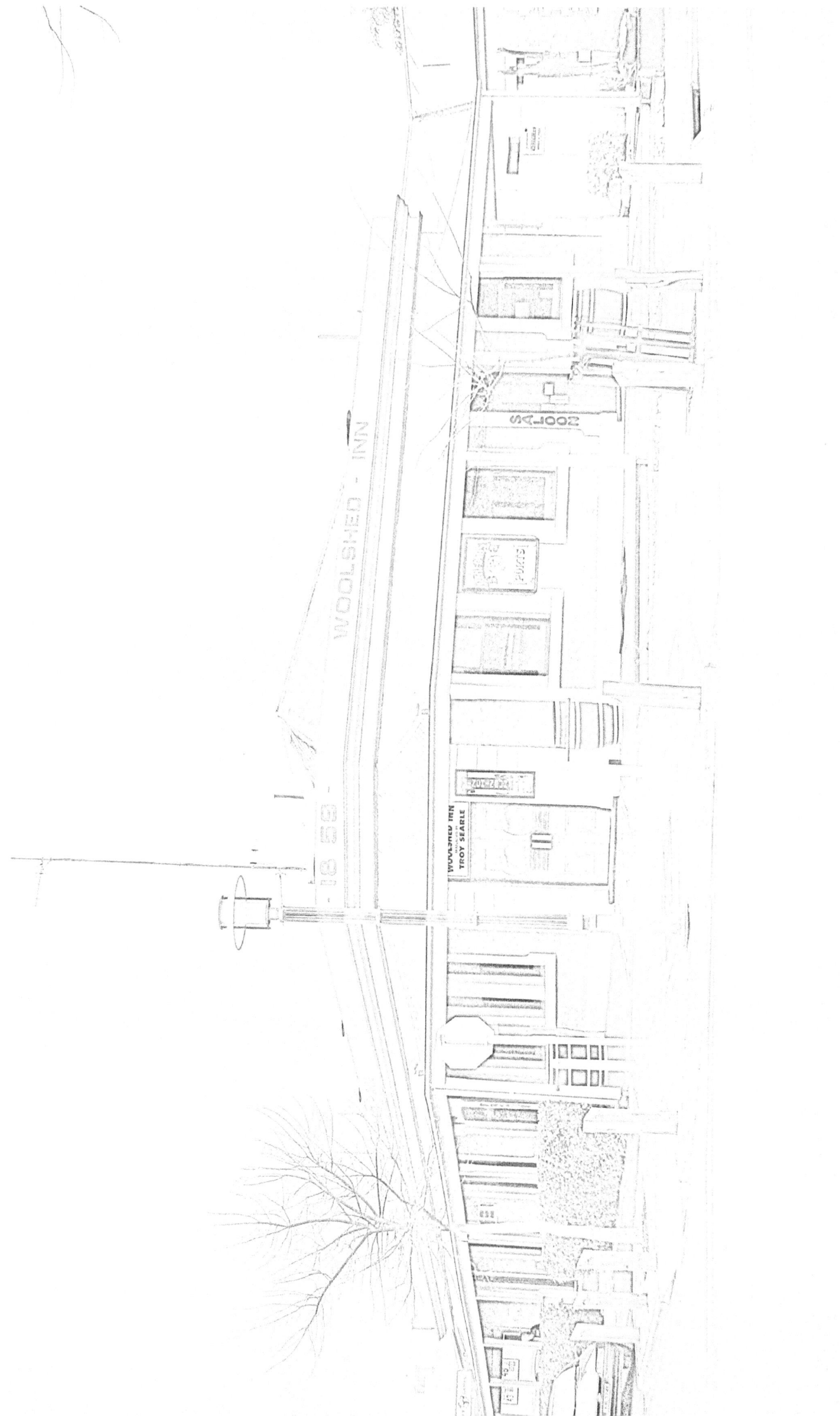

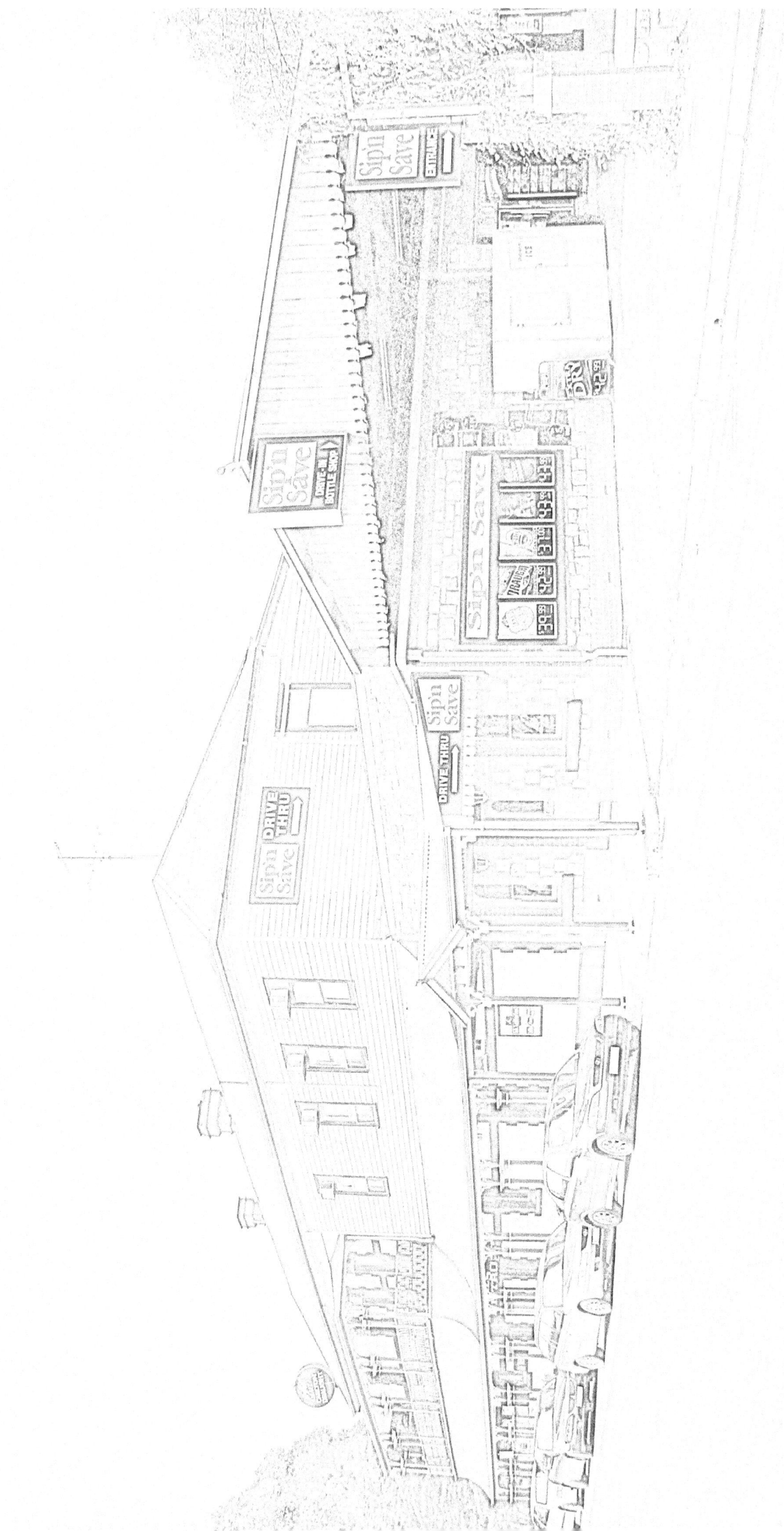

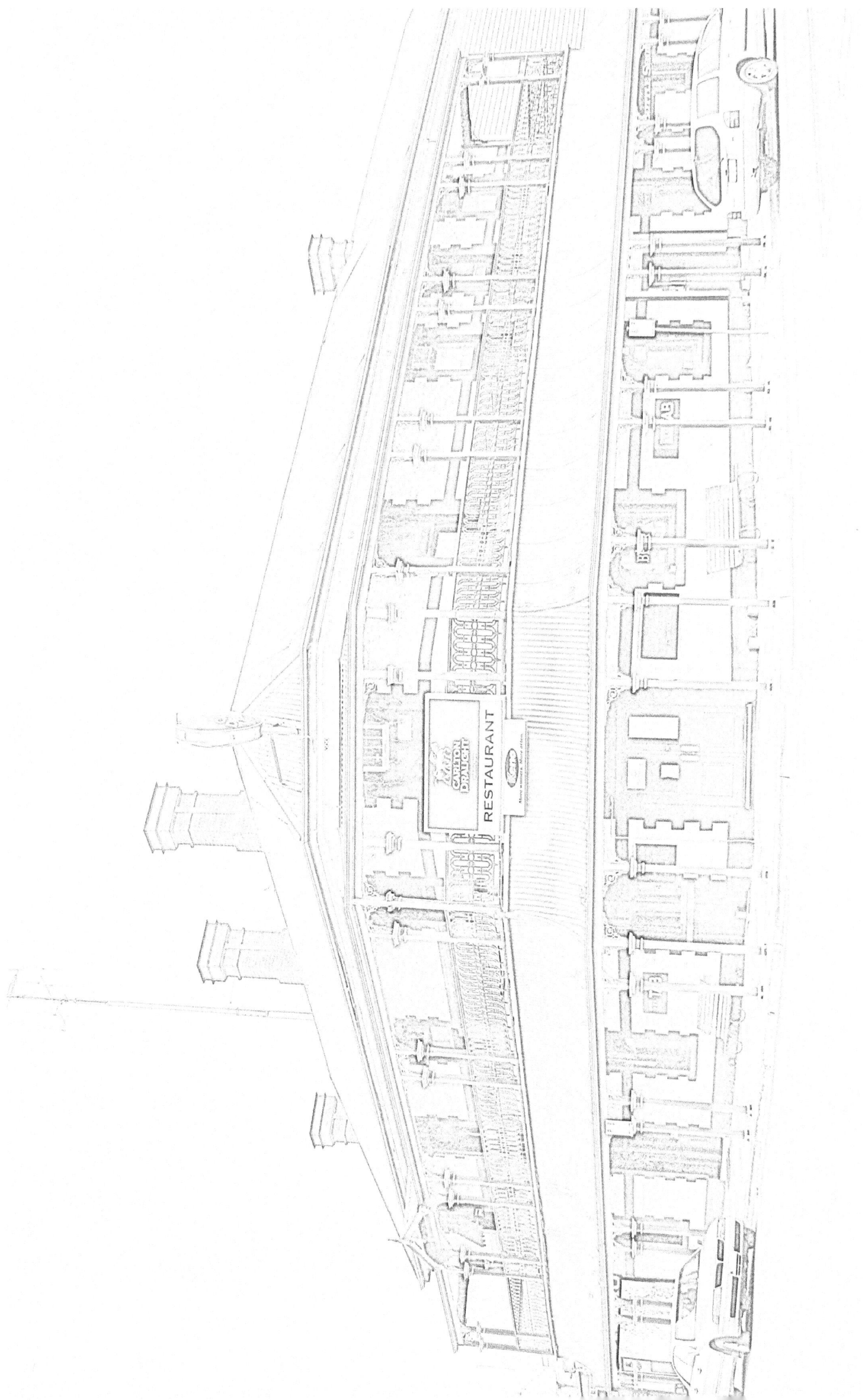

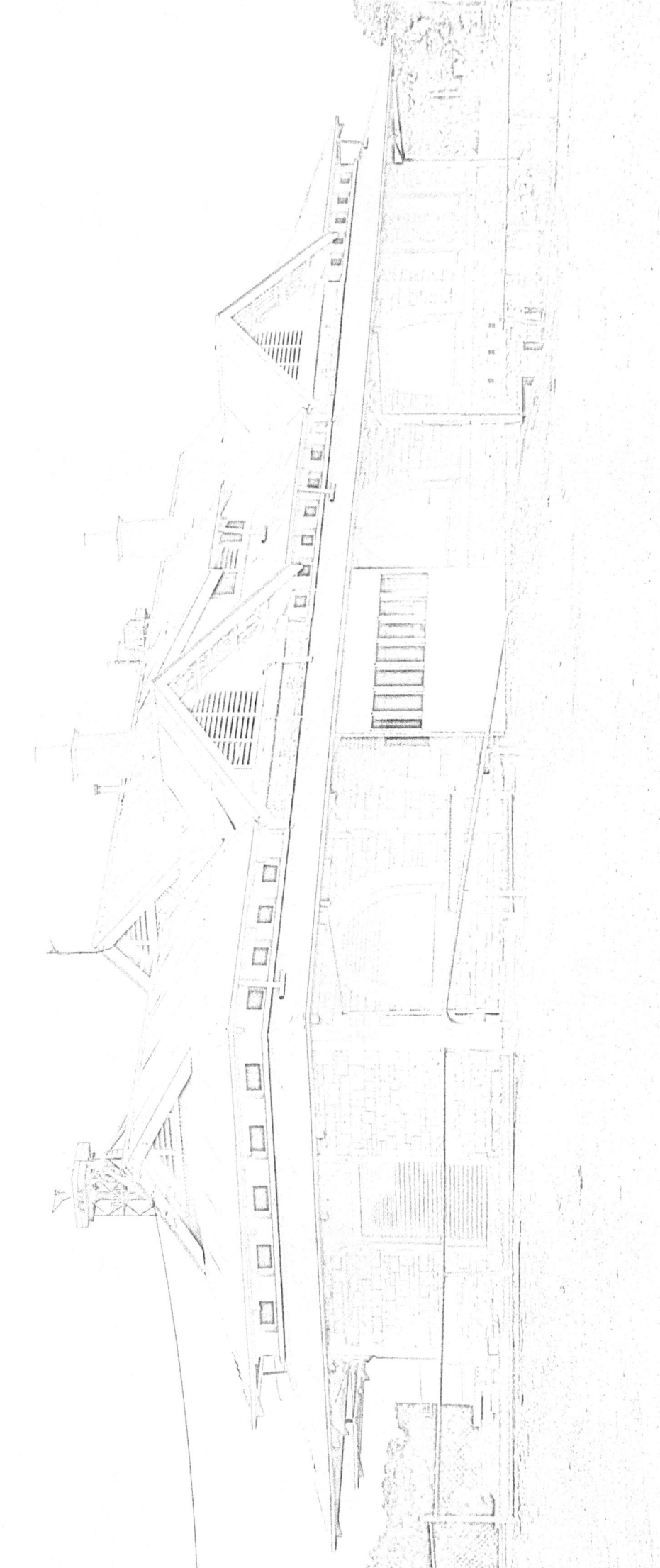

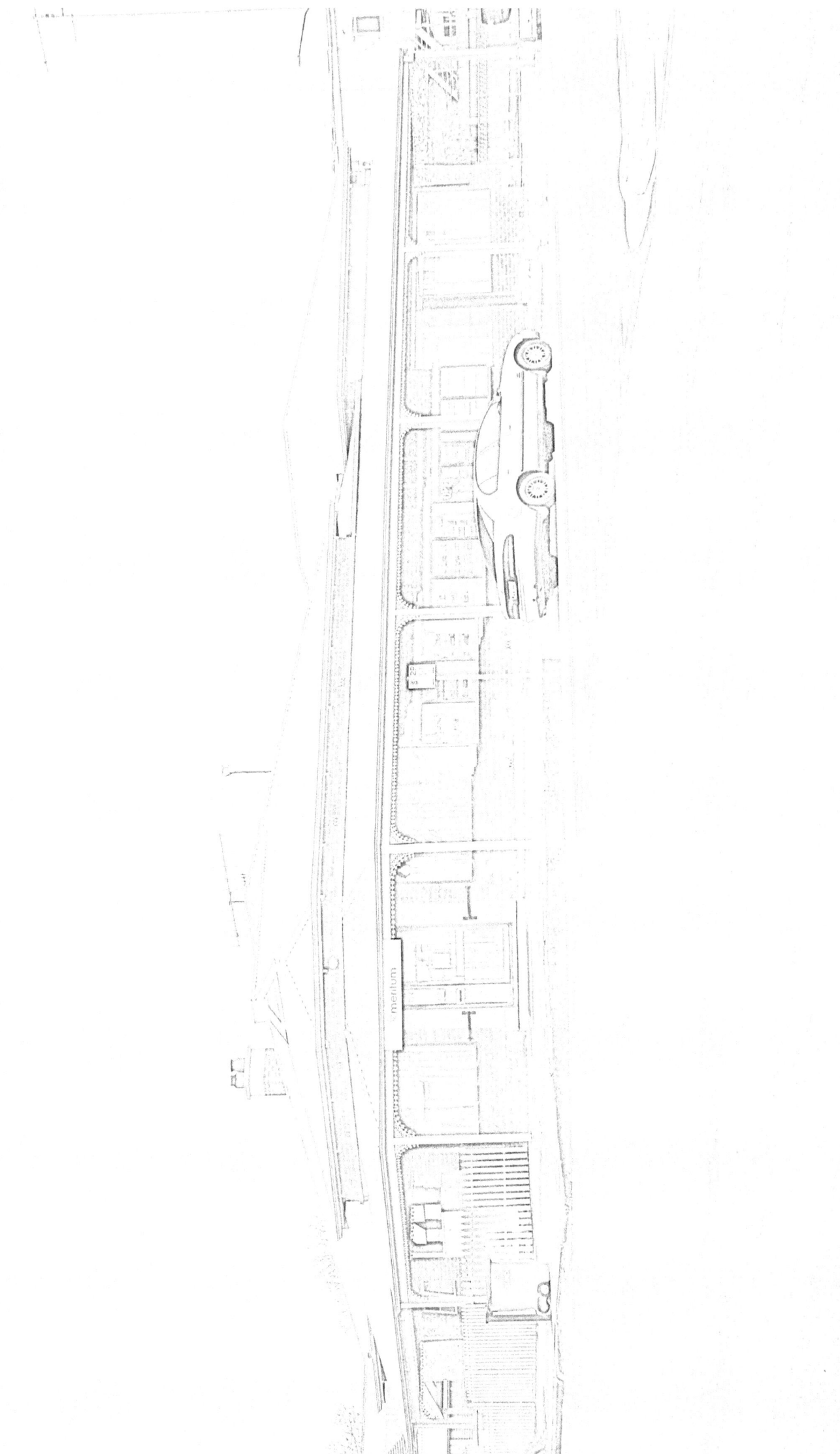

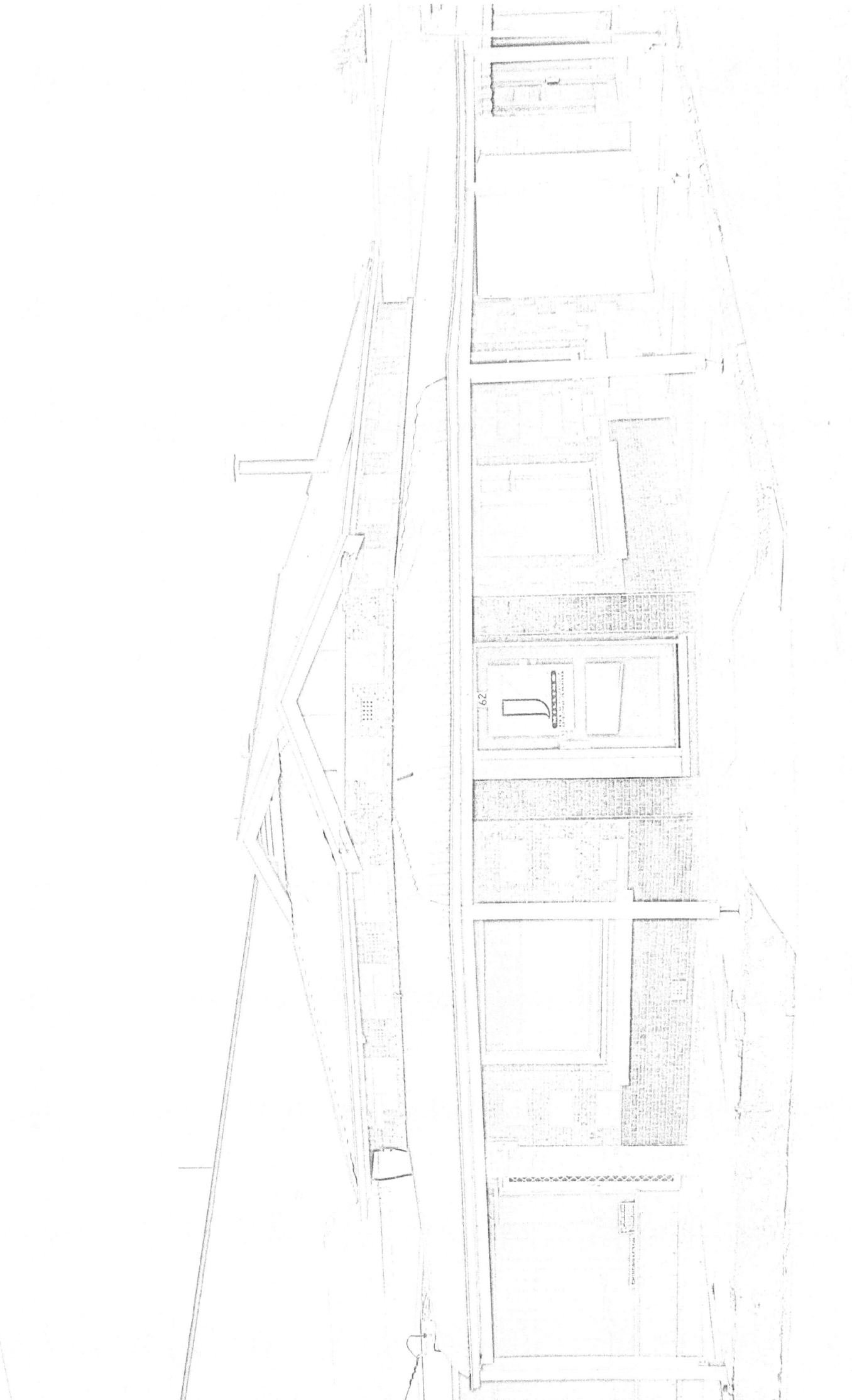

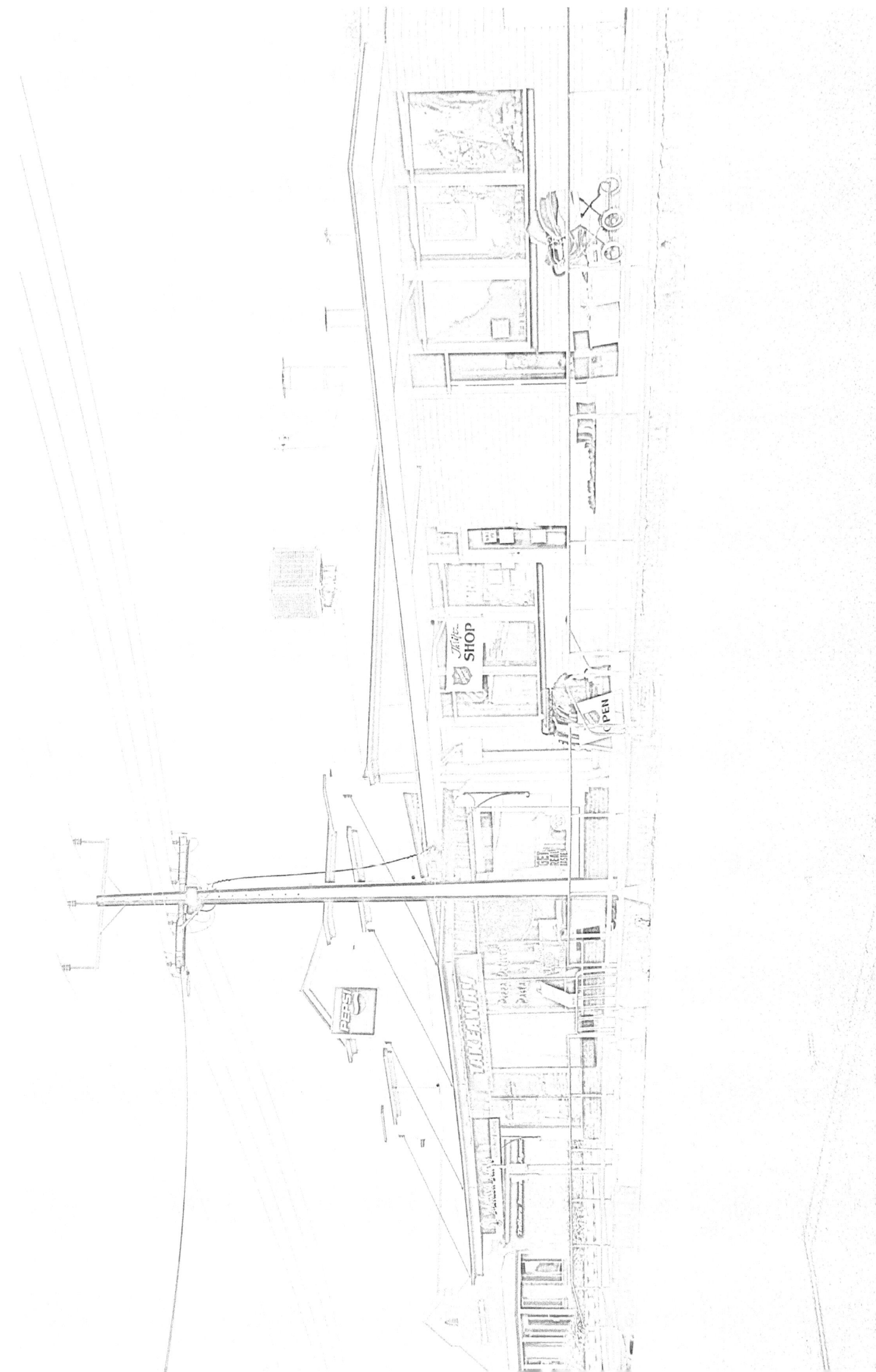

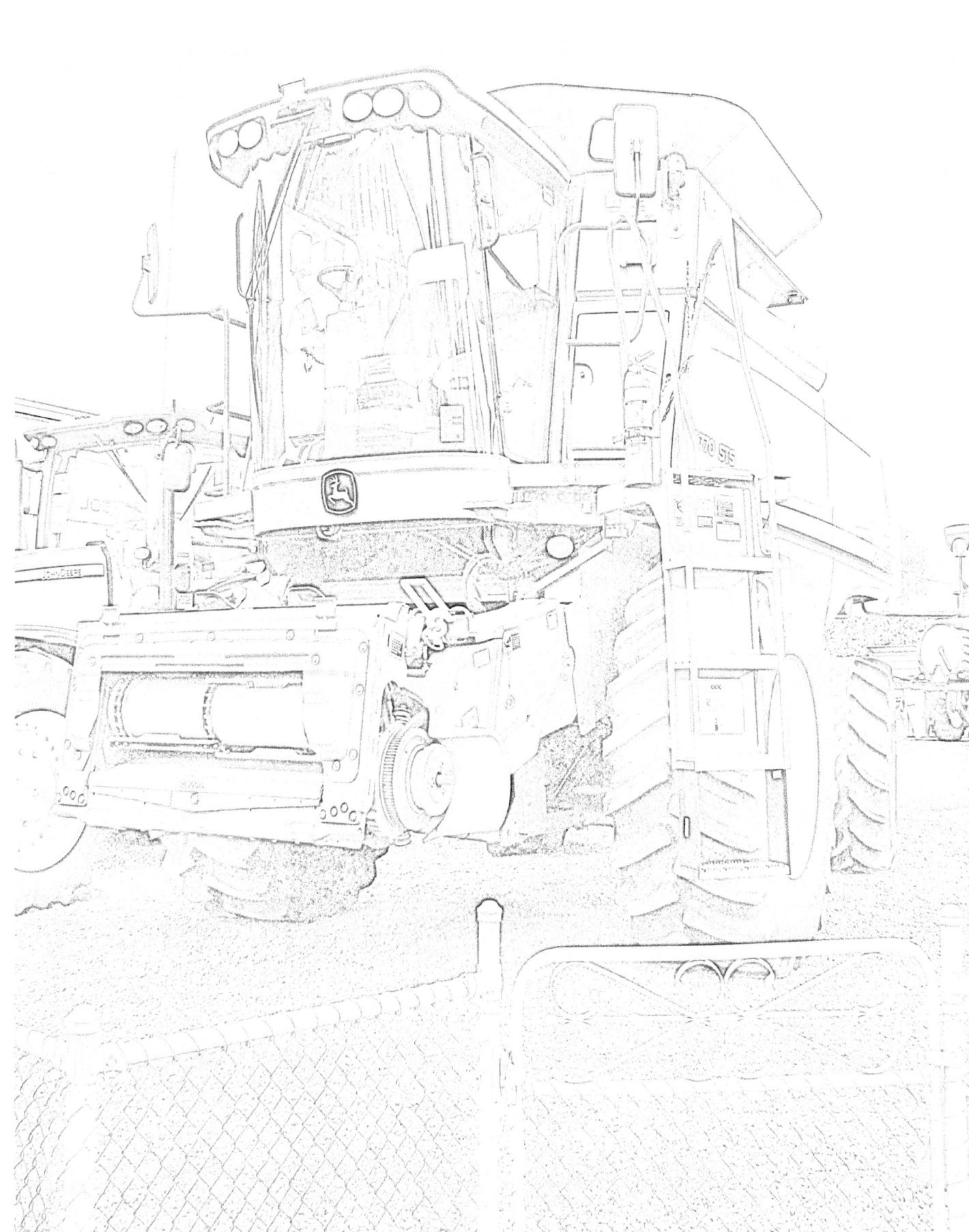